This coloring book belongs to.

First Edition: 2020

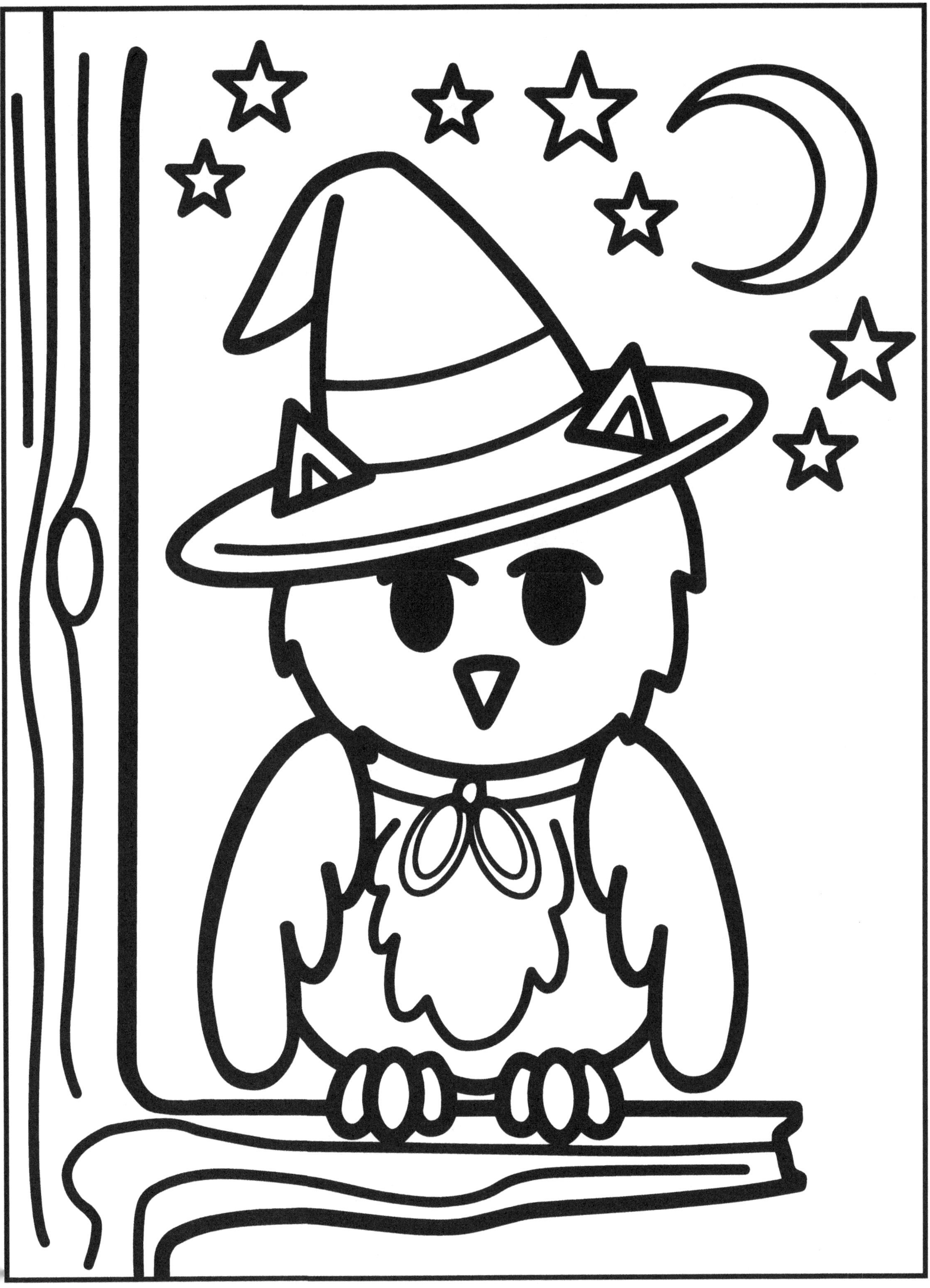

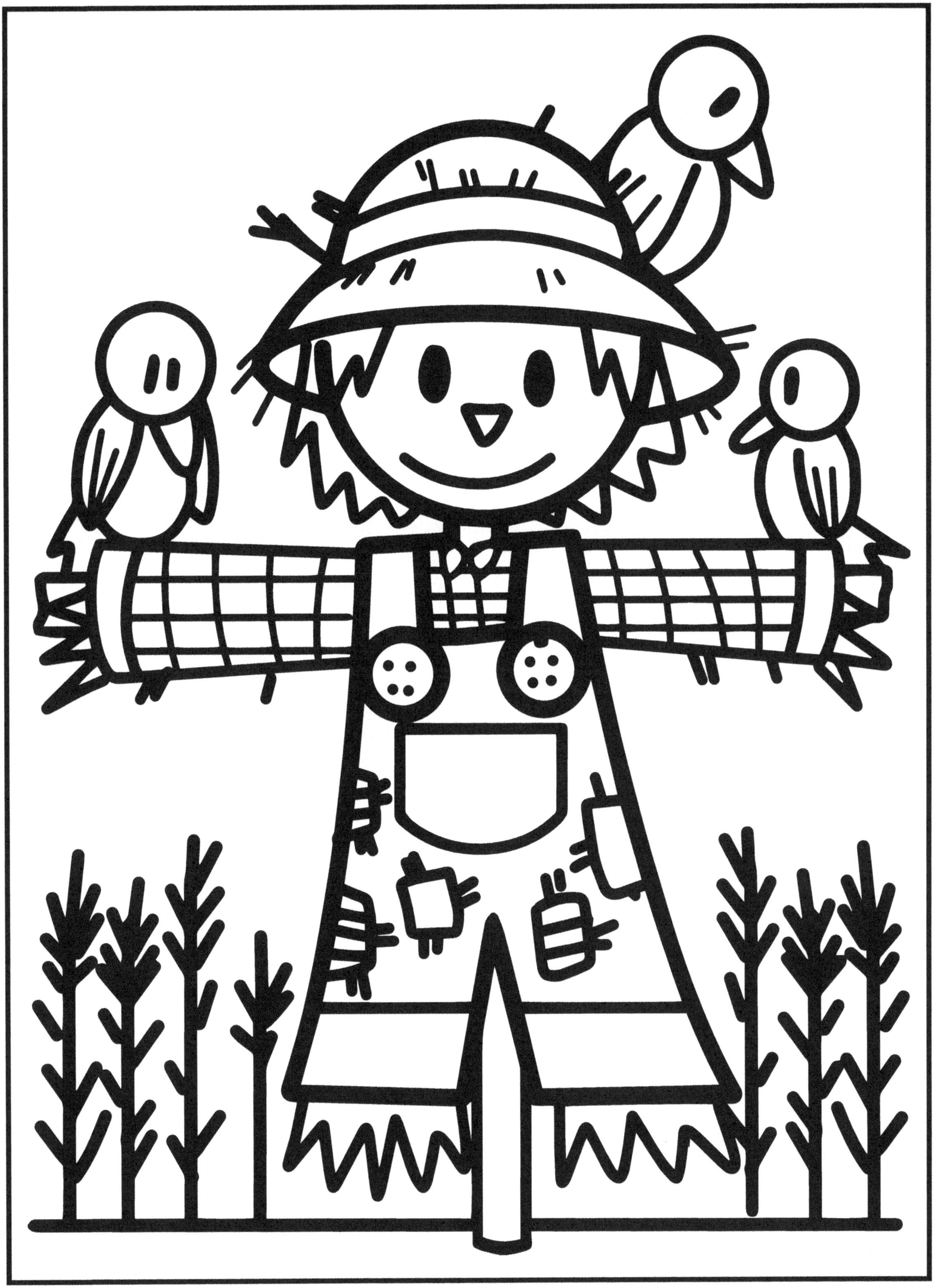

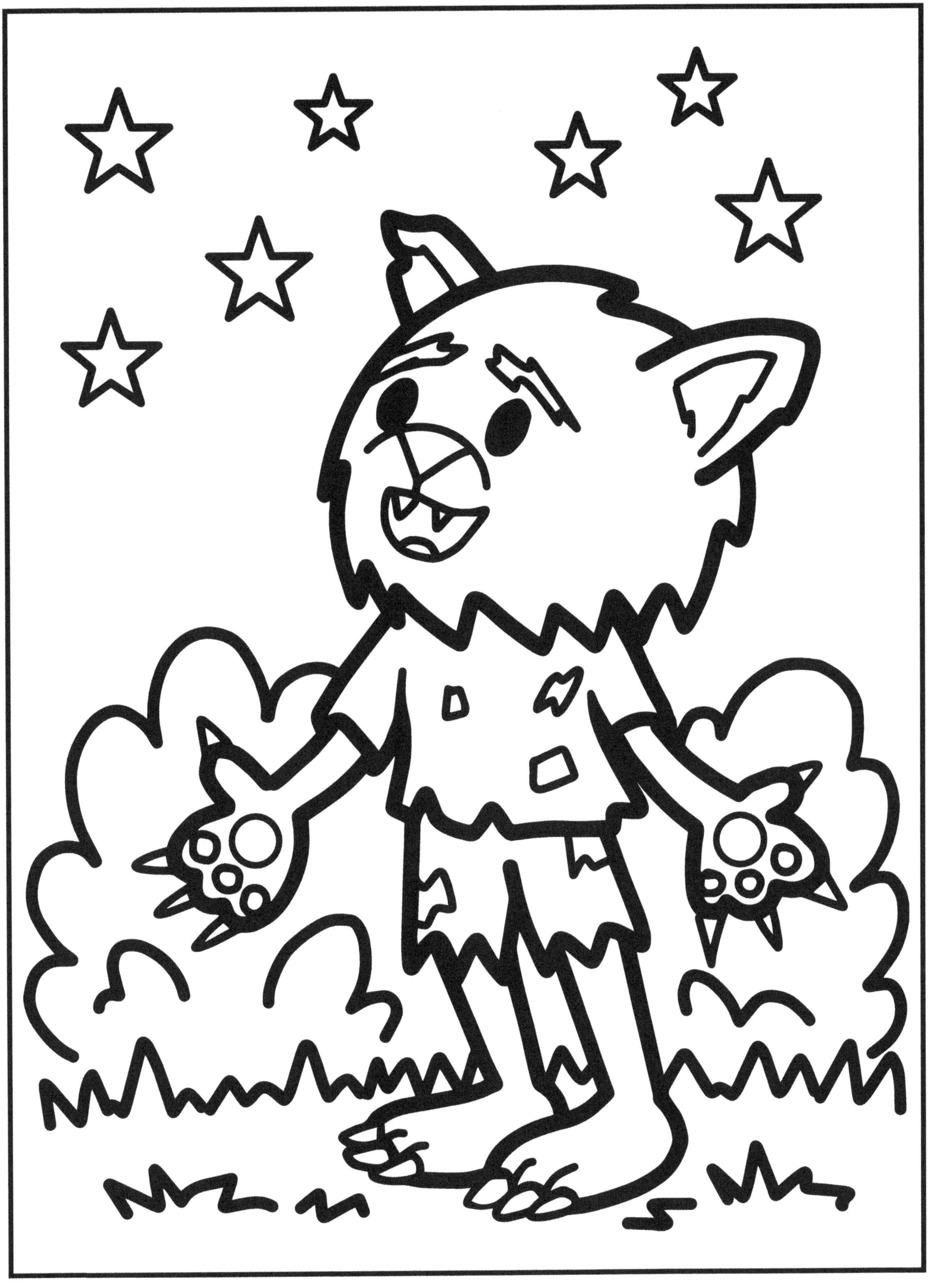

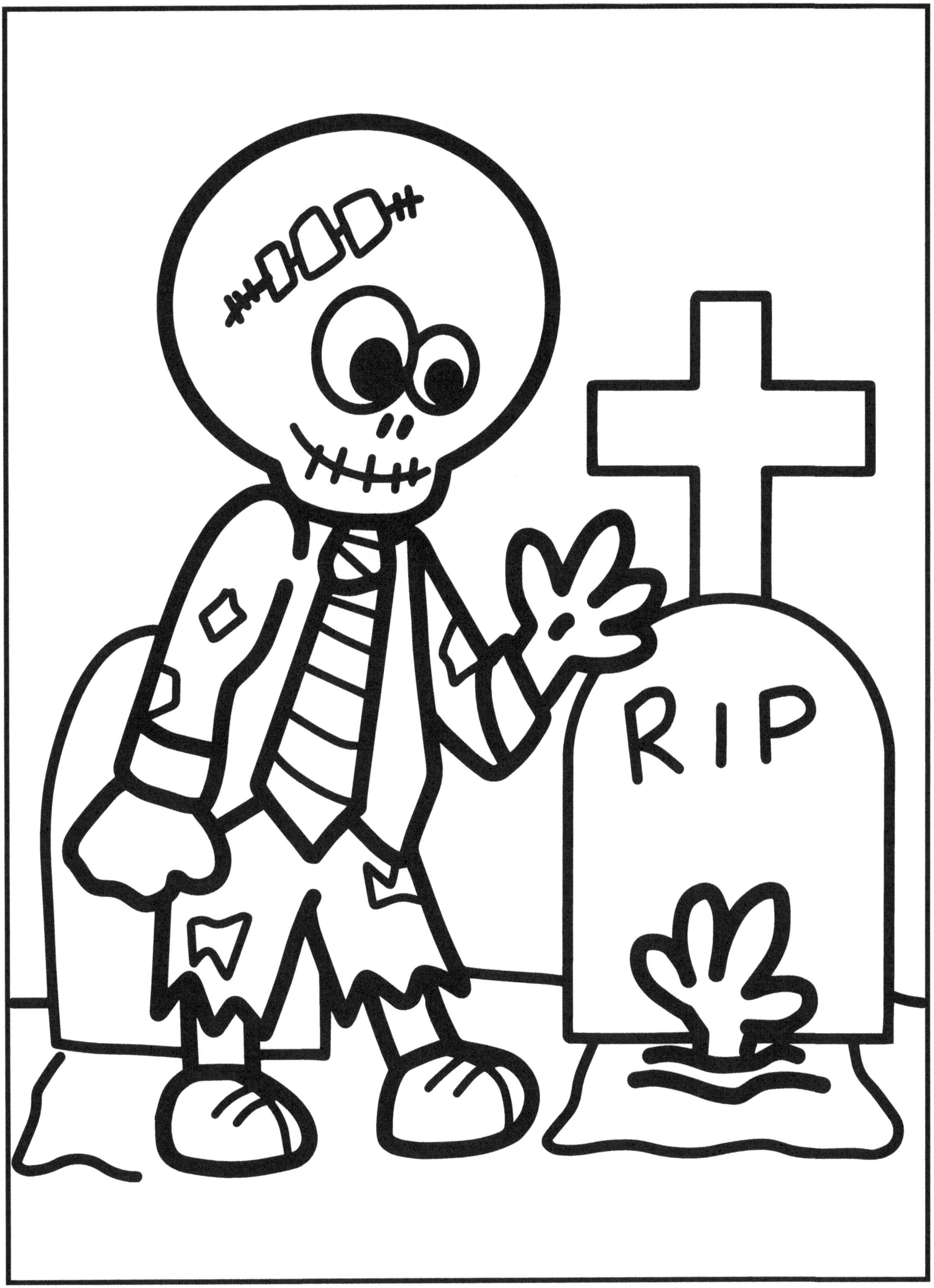
RIP

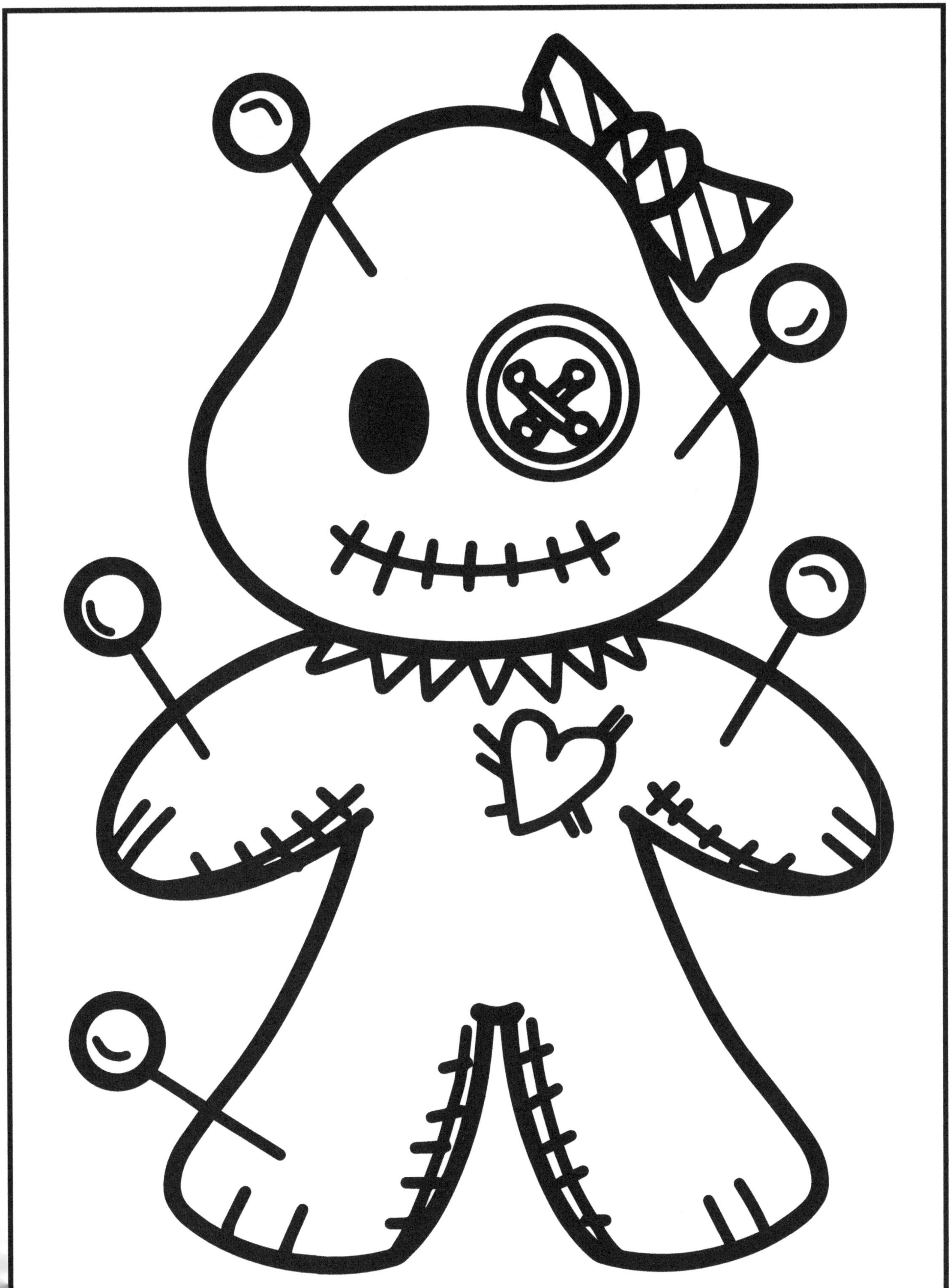

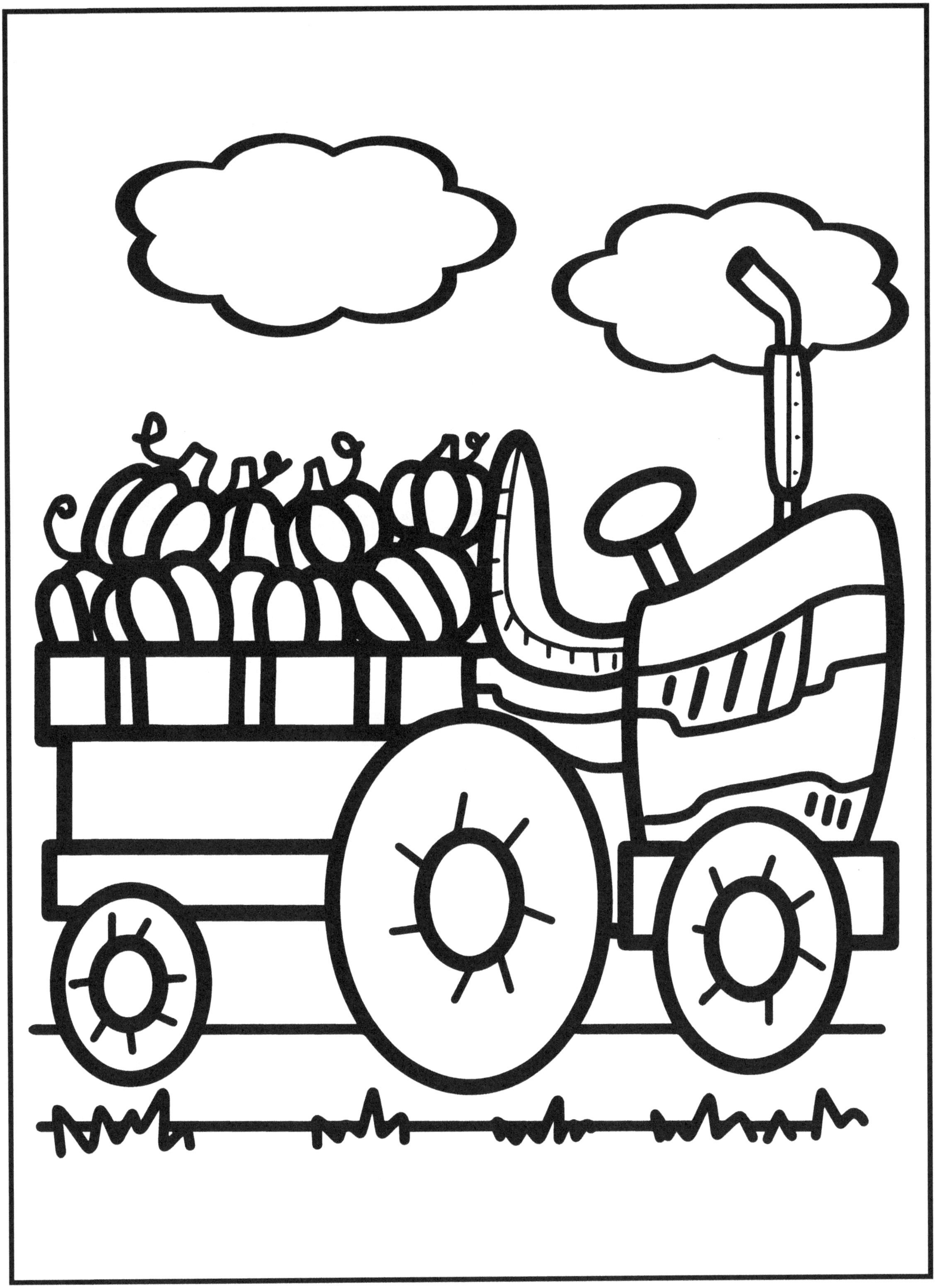

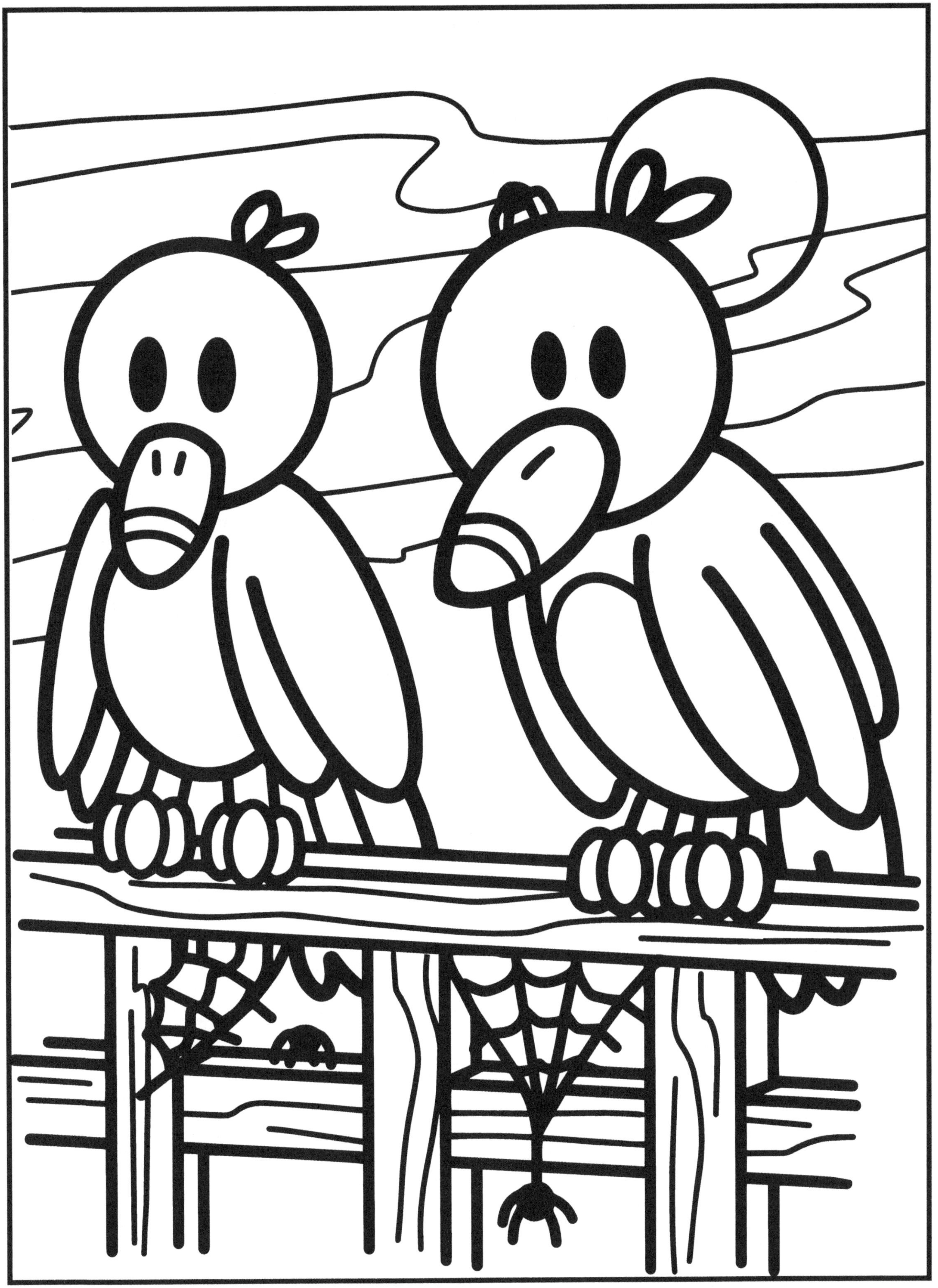

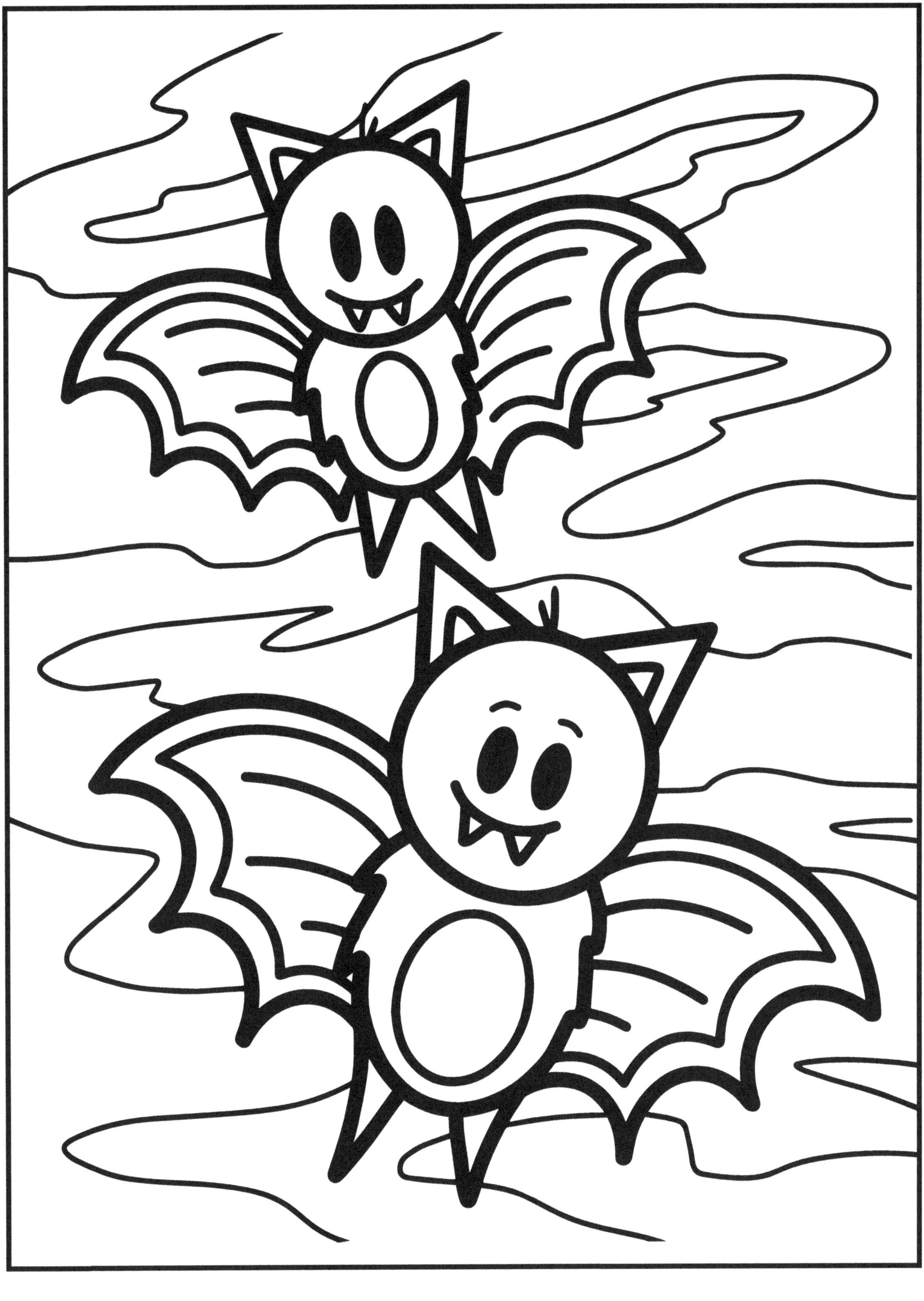

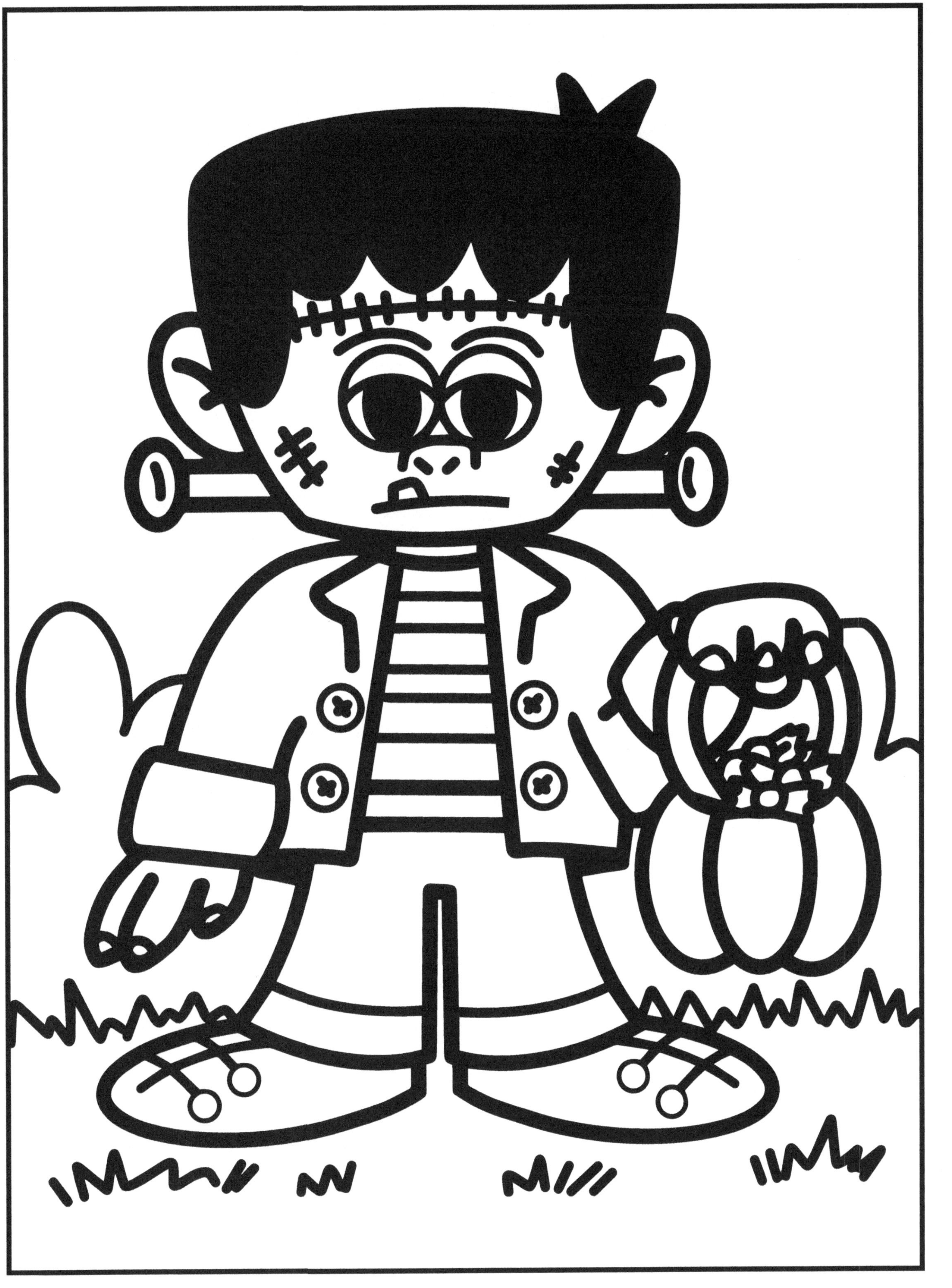

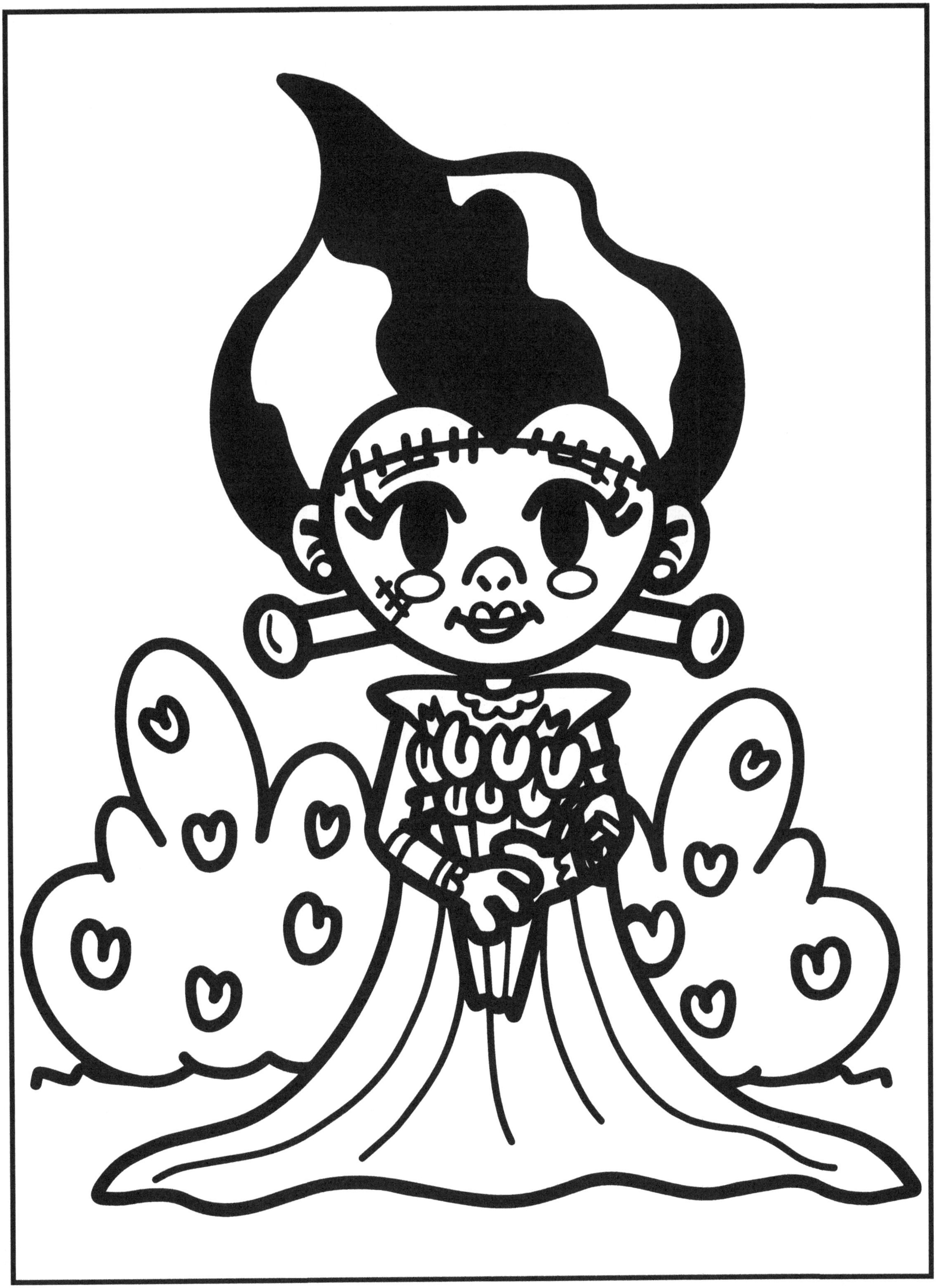

RIP
RIP

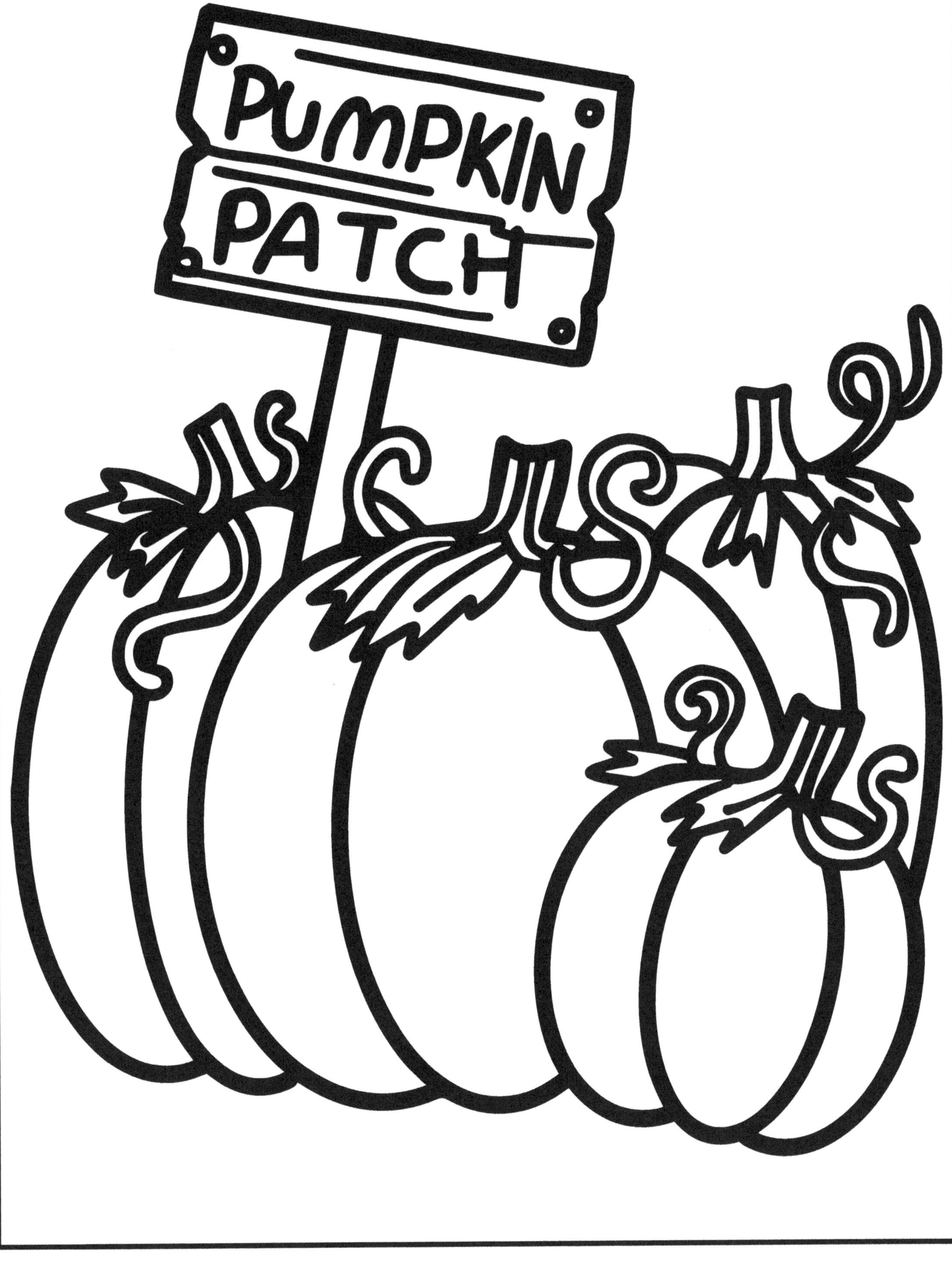
PUMPKIN
PATCH

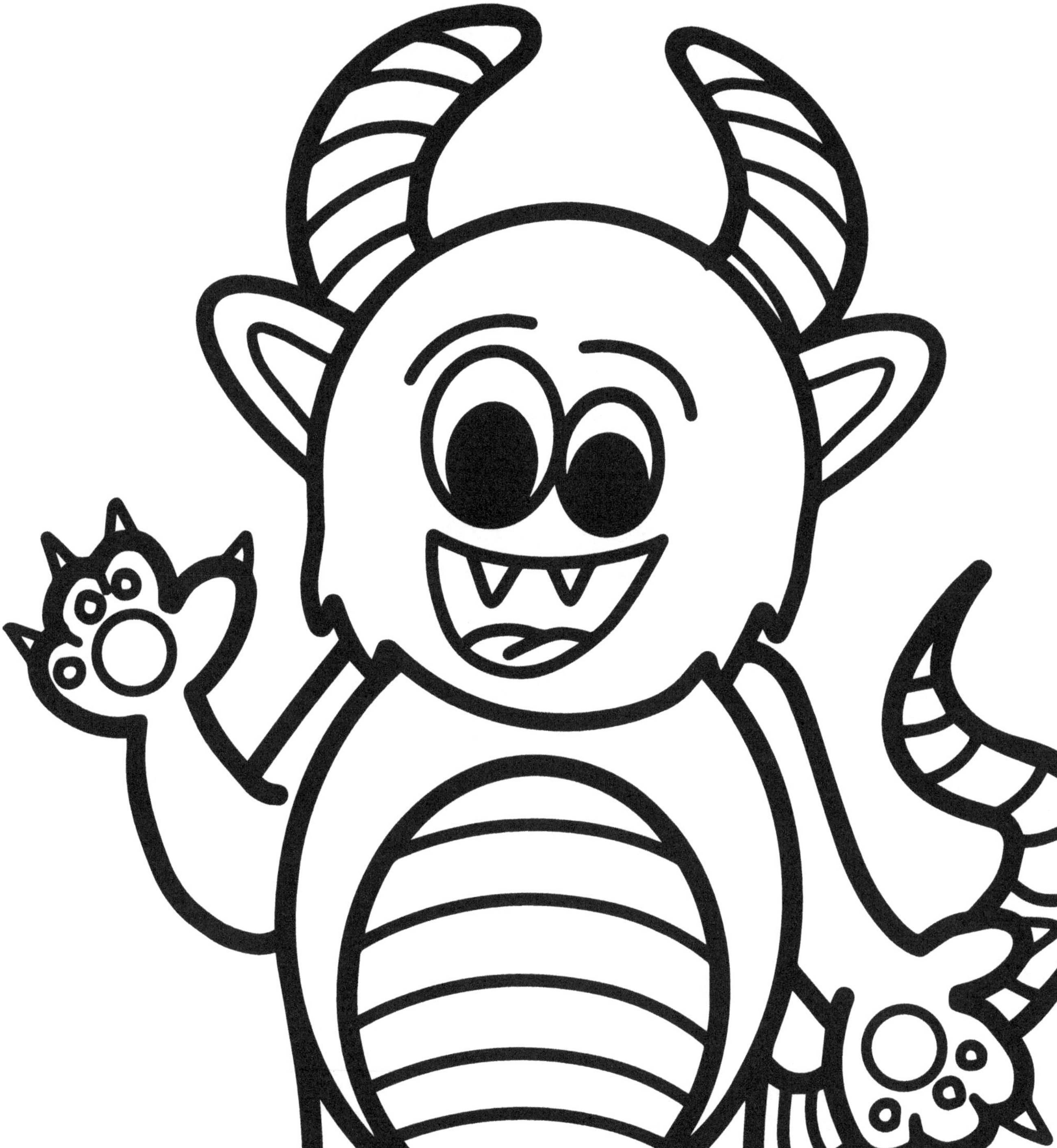

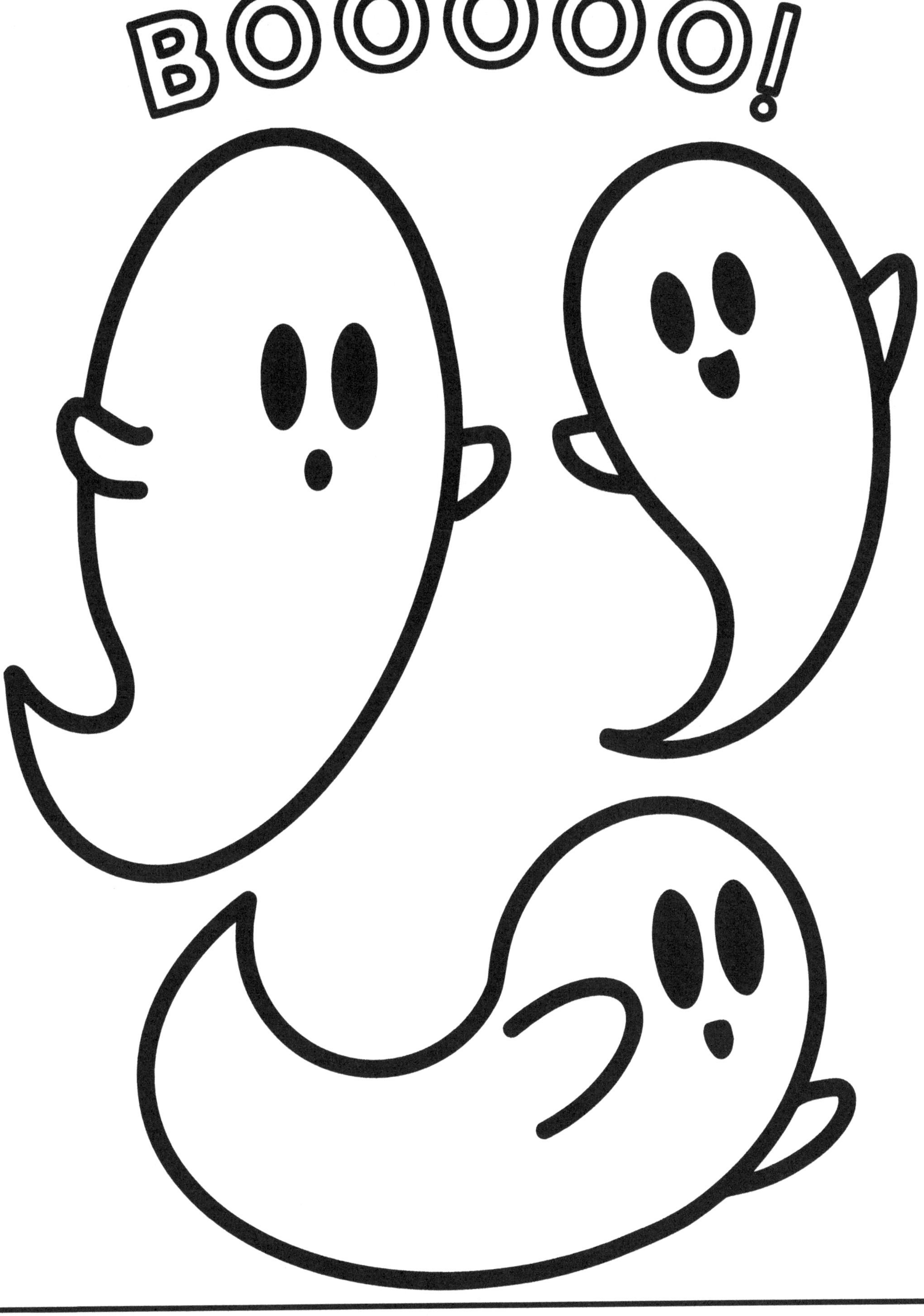
BOOOOO!

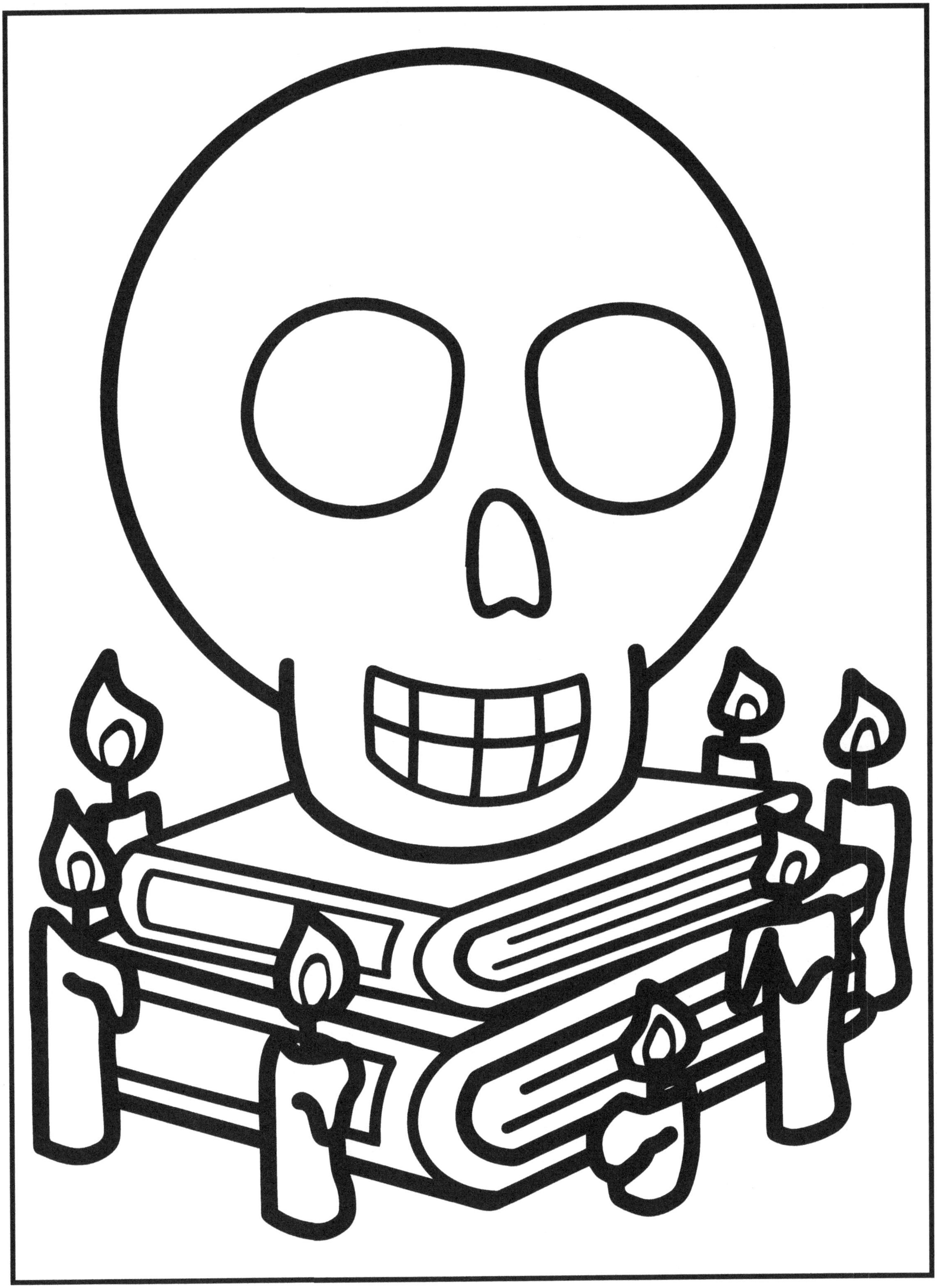

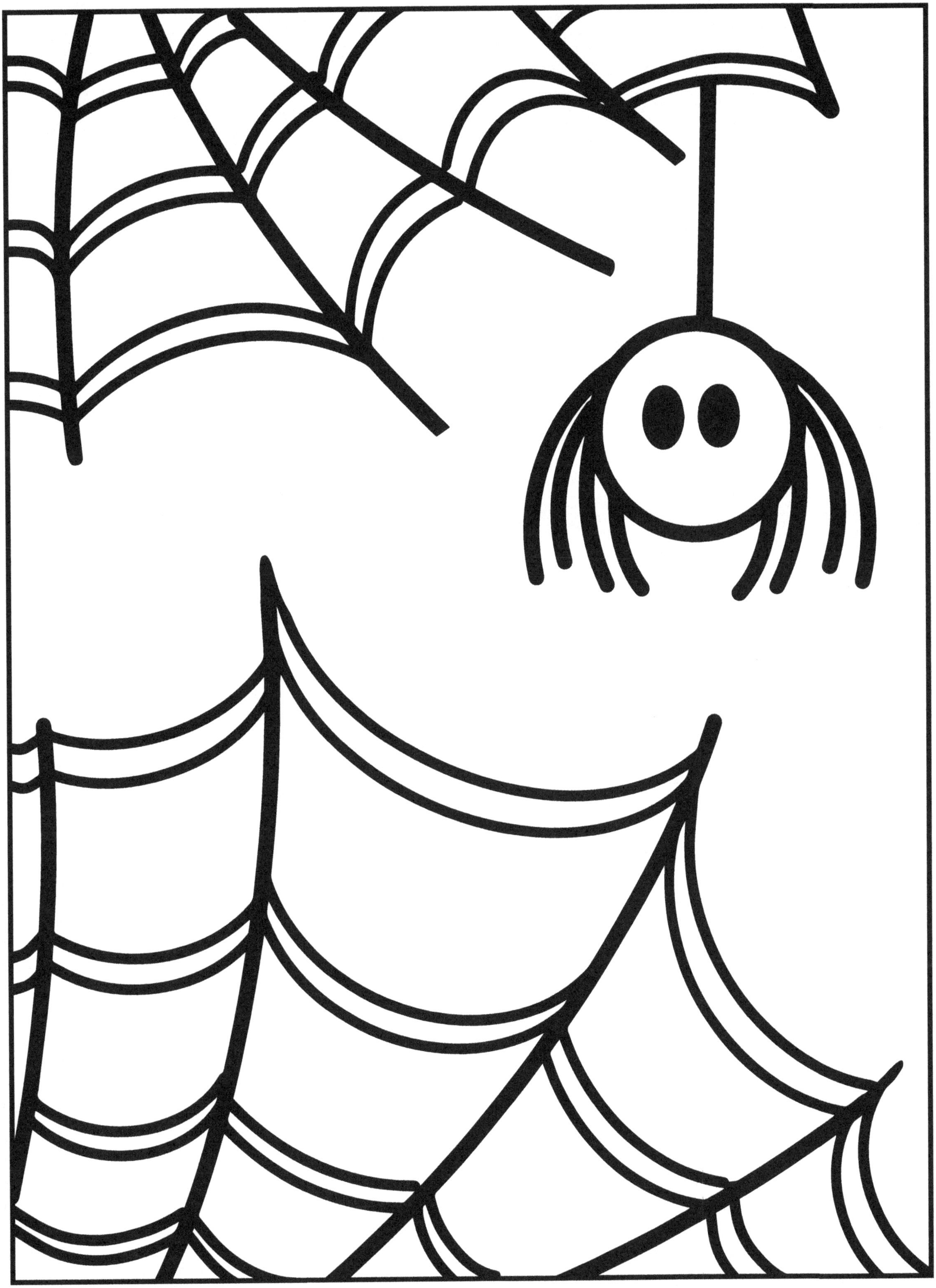

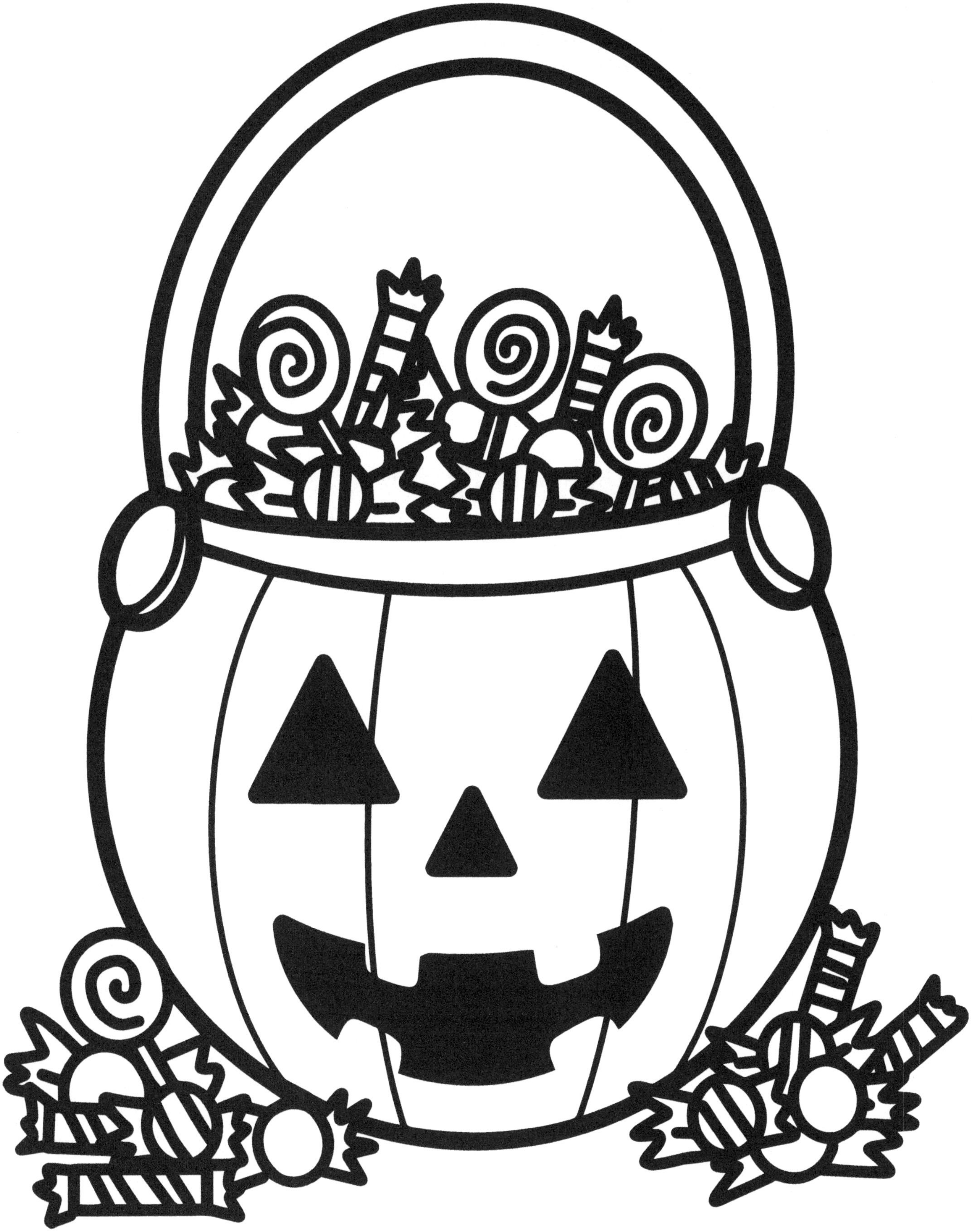

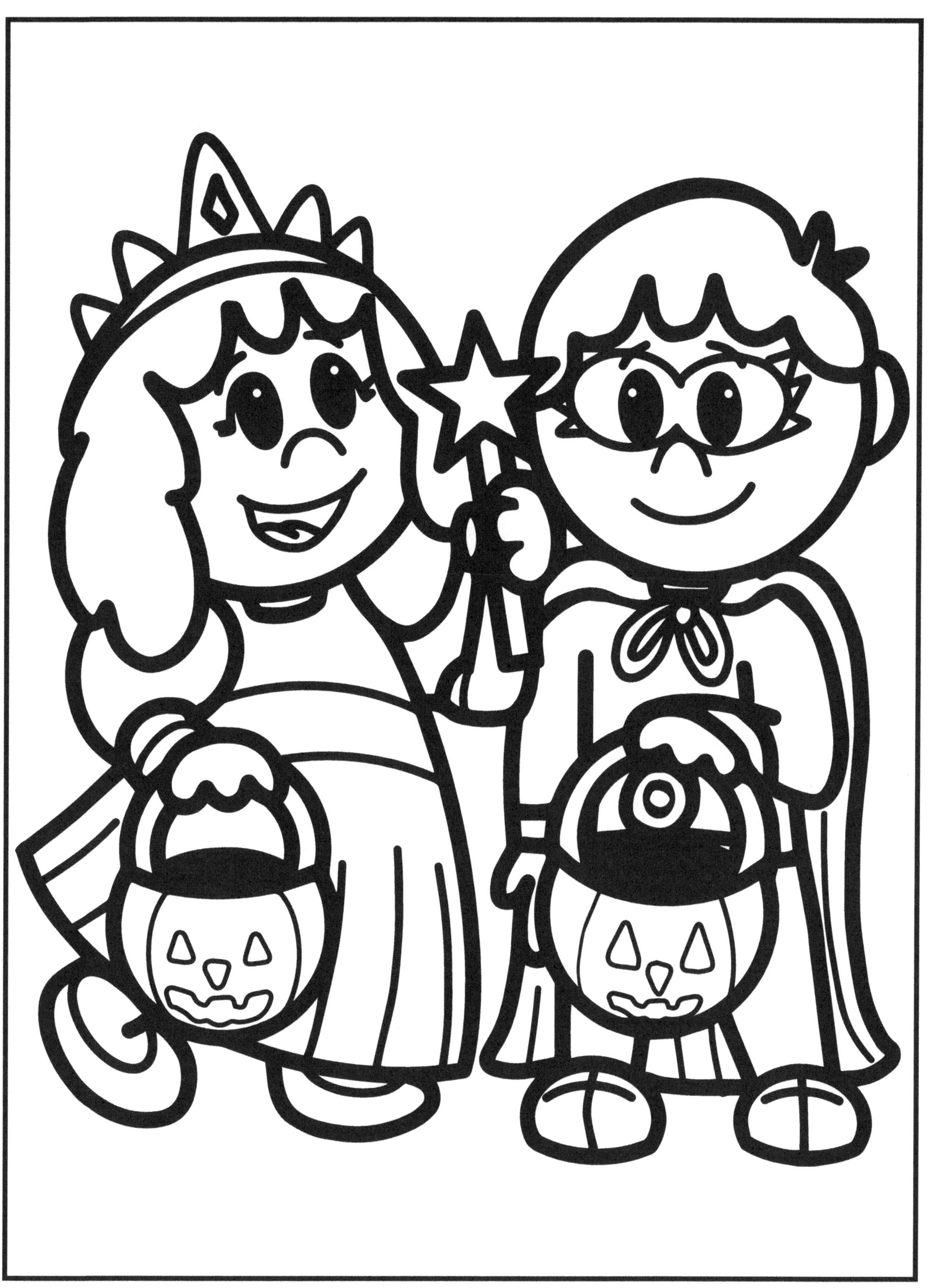

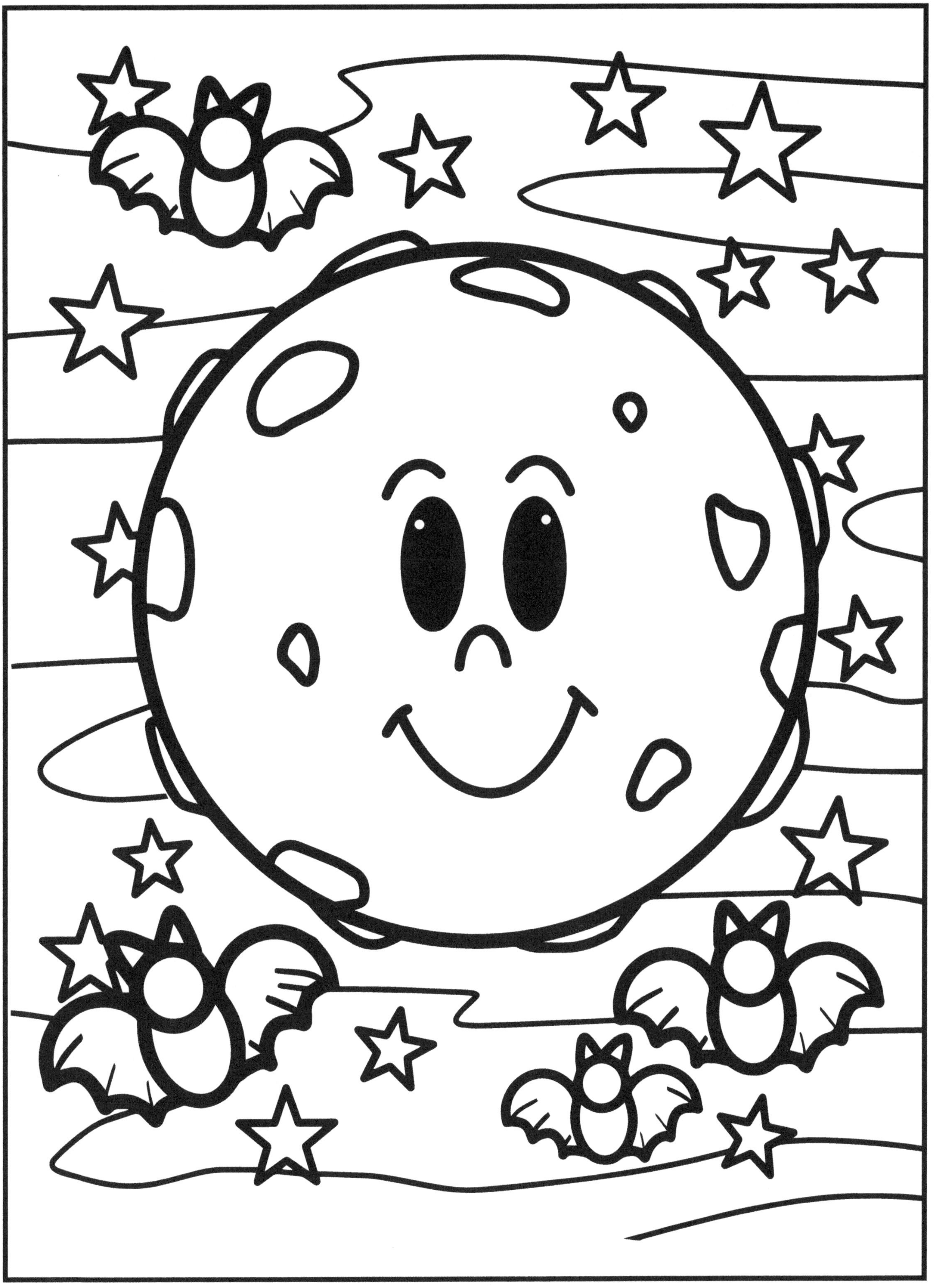

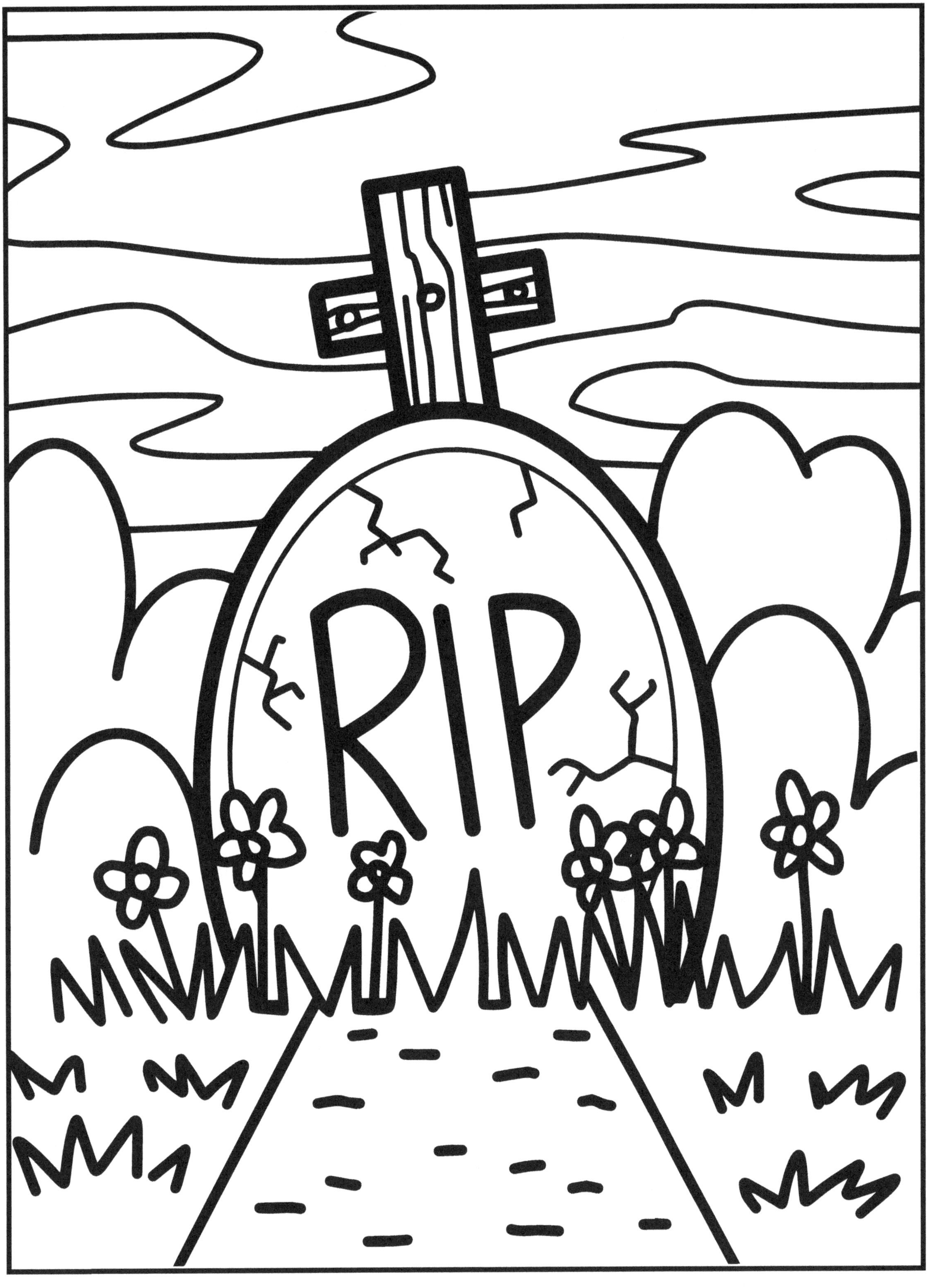
RIP

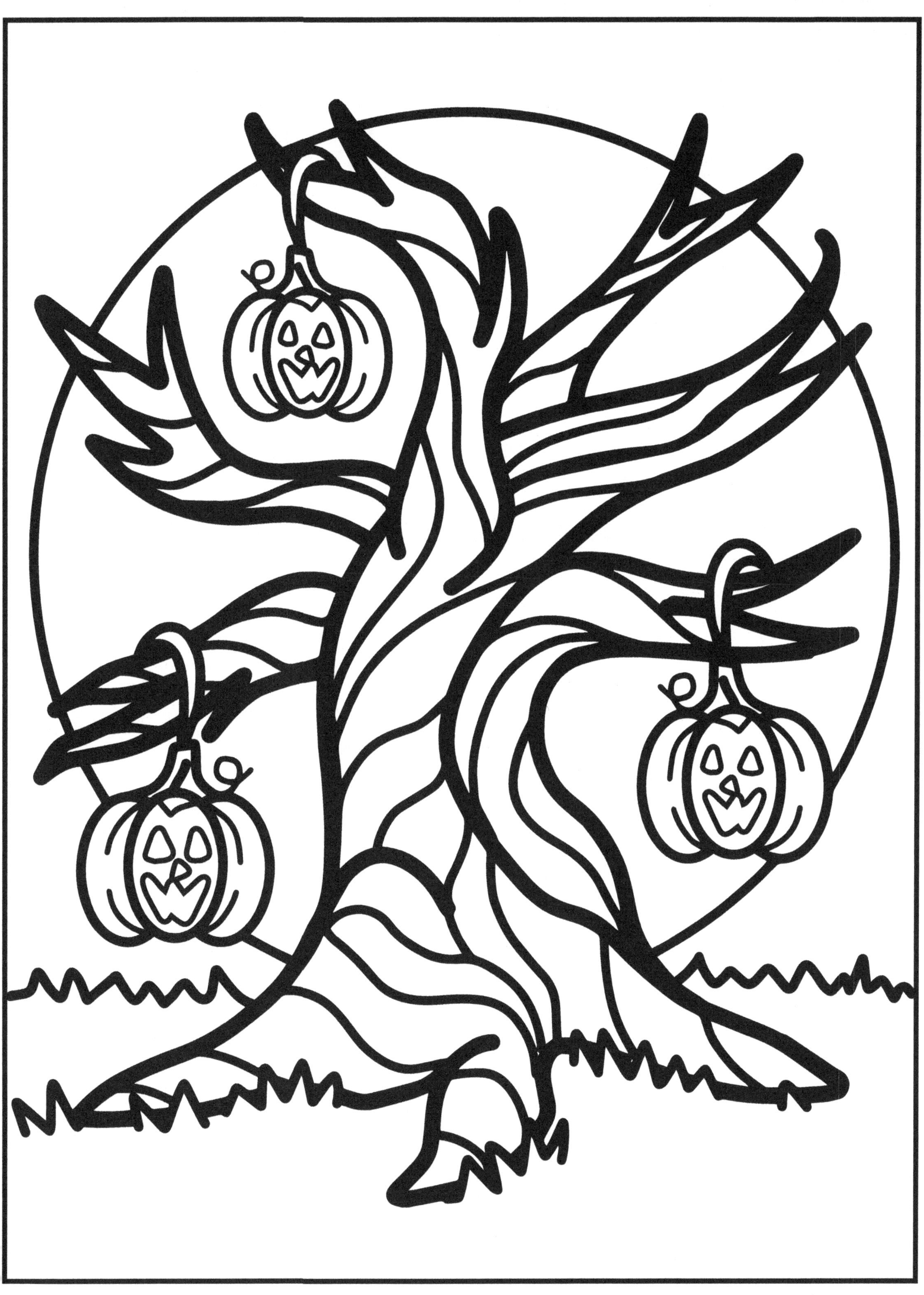

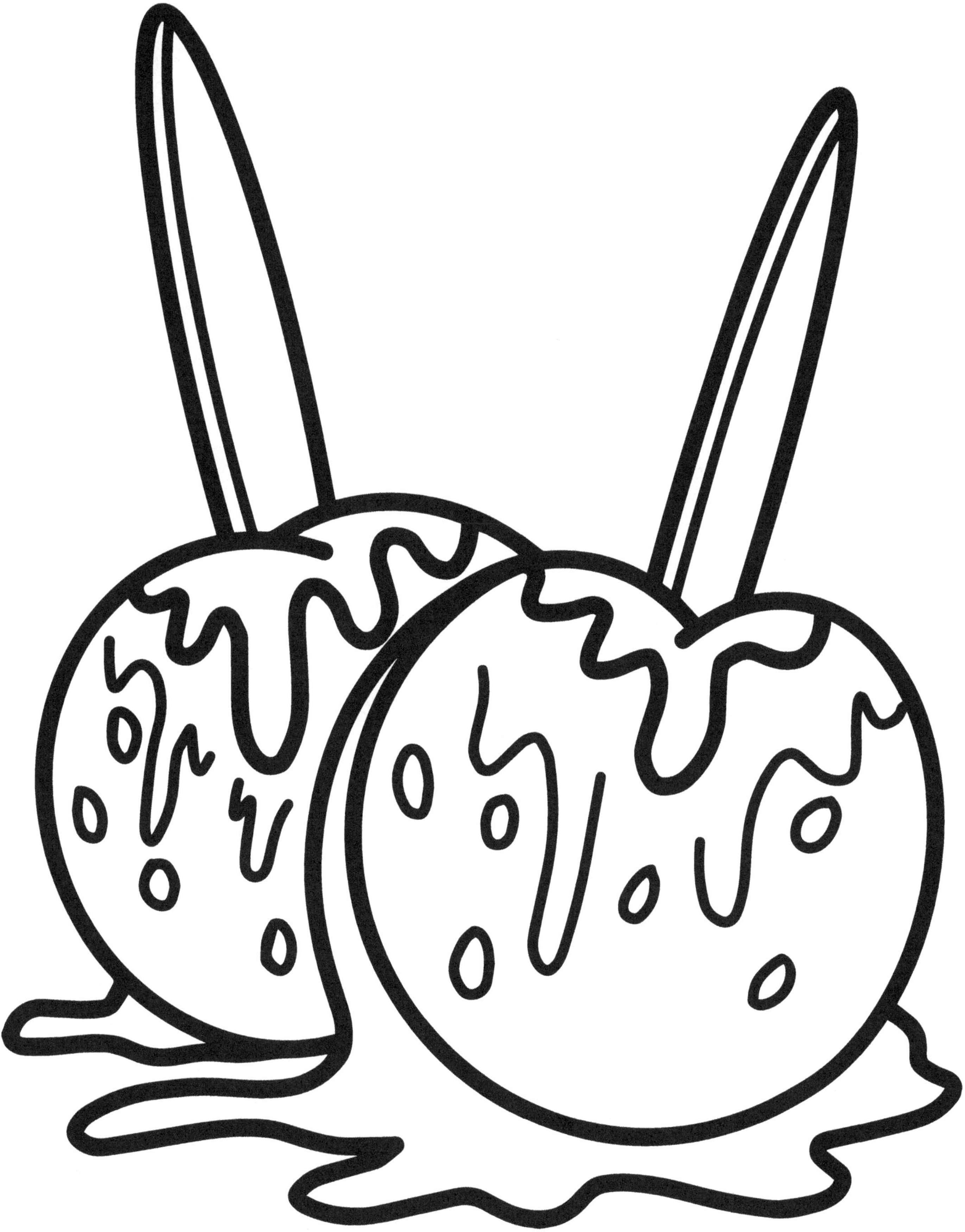

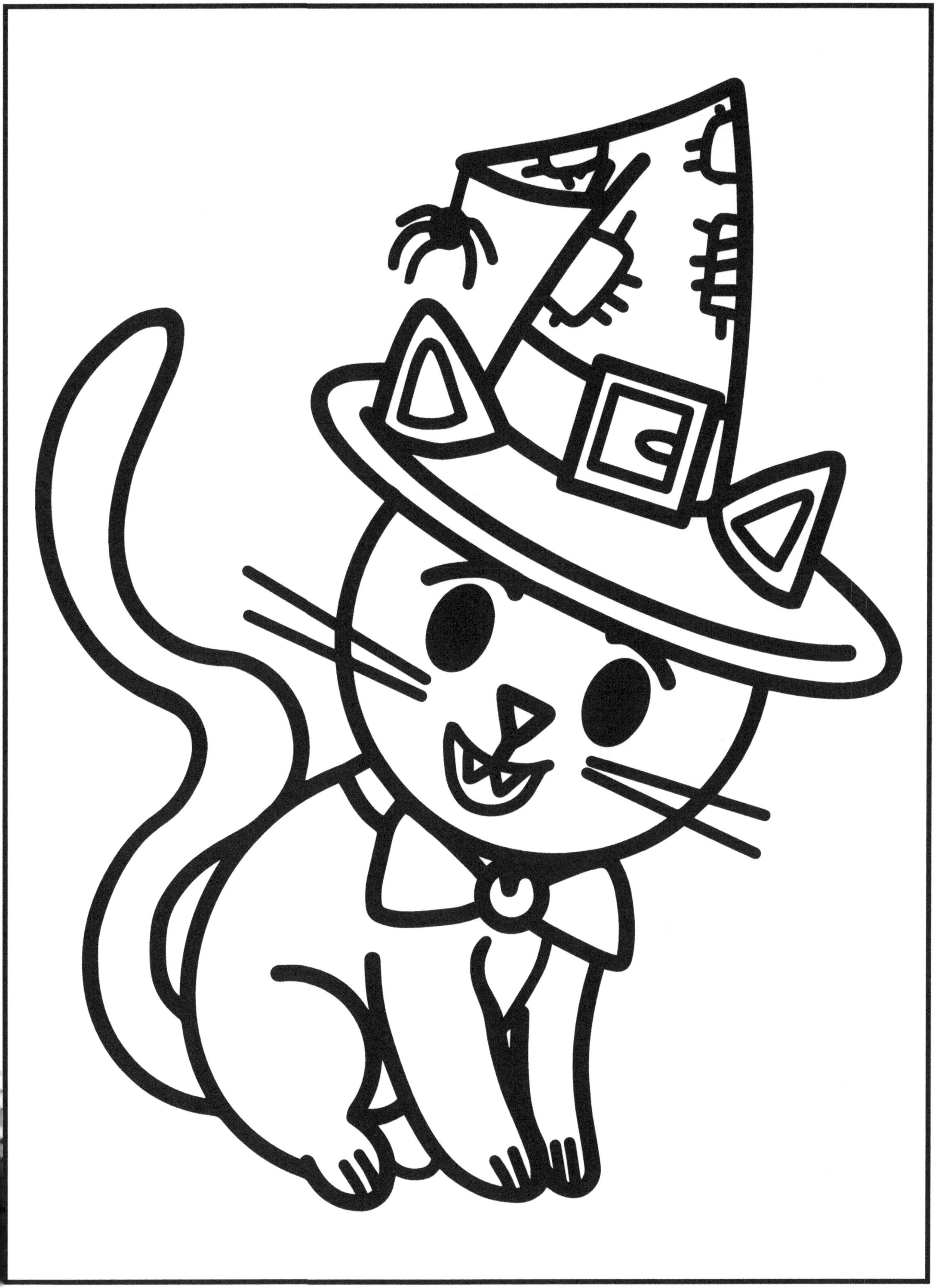

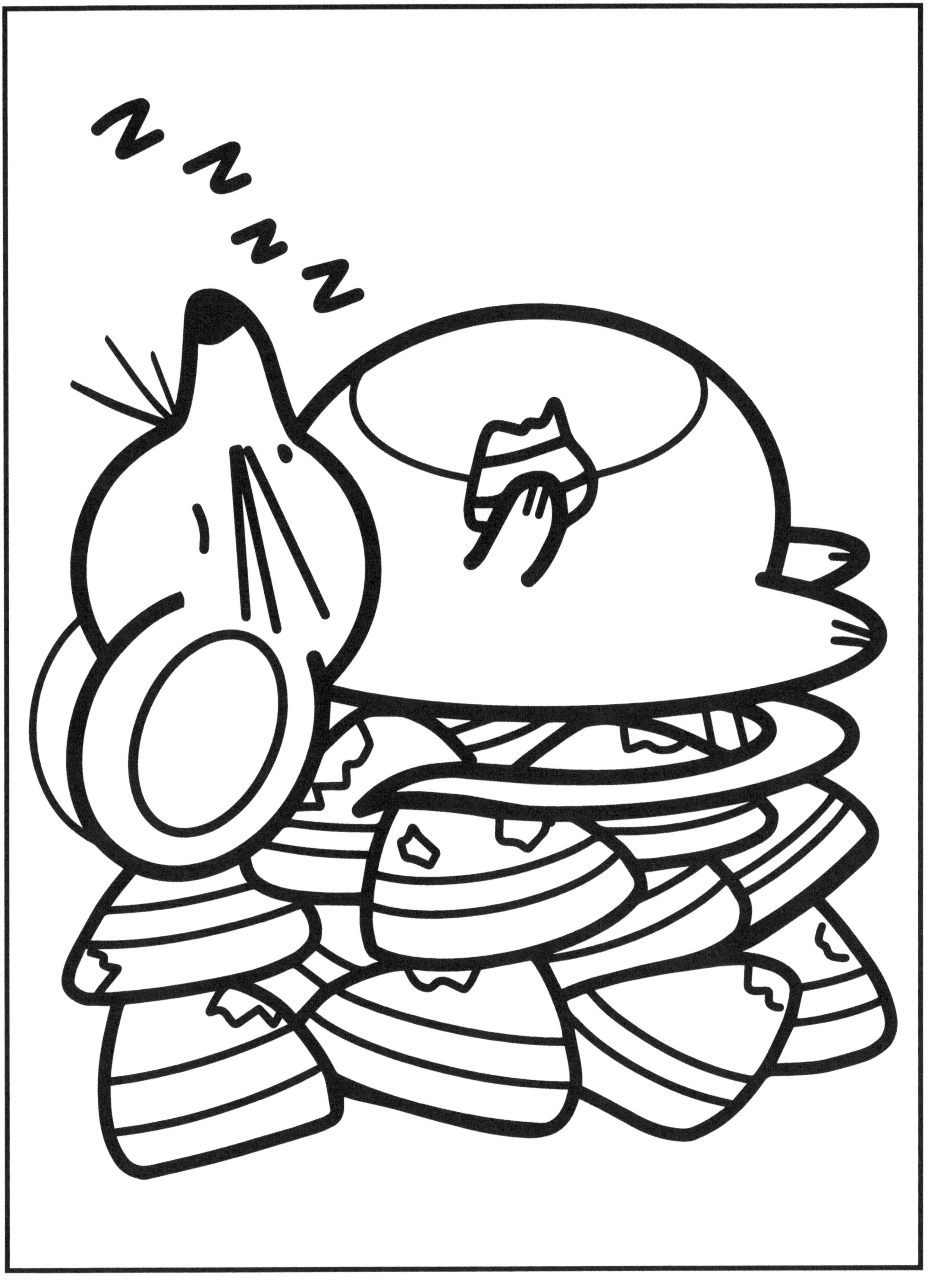
Z Z Z Z

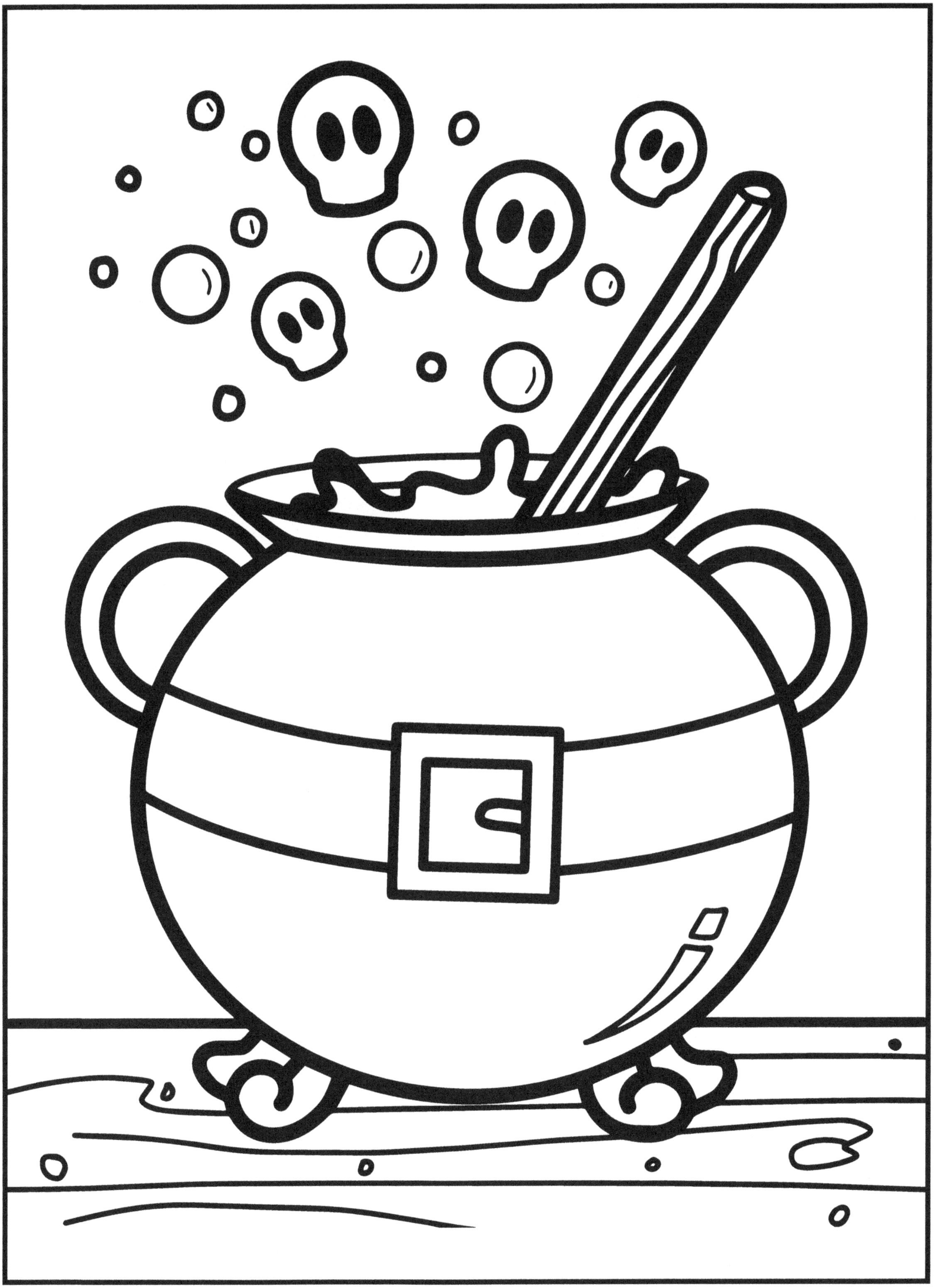

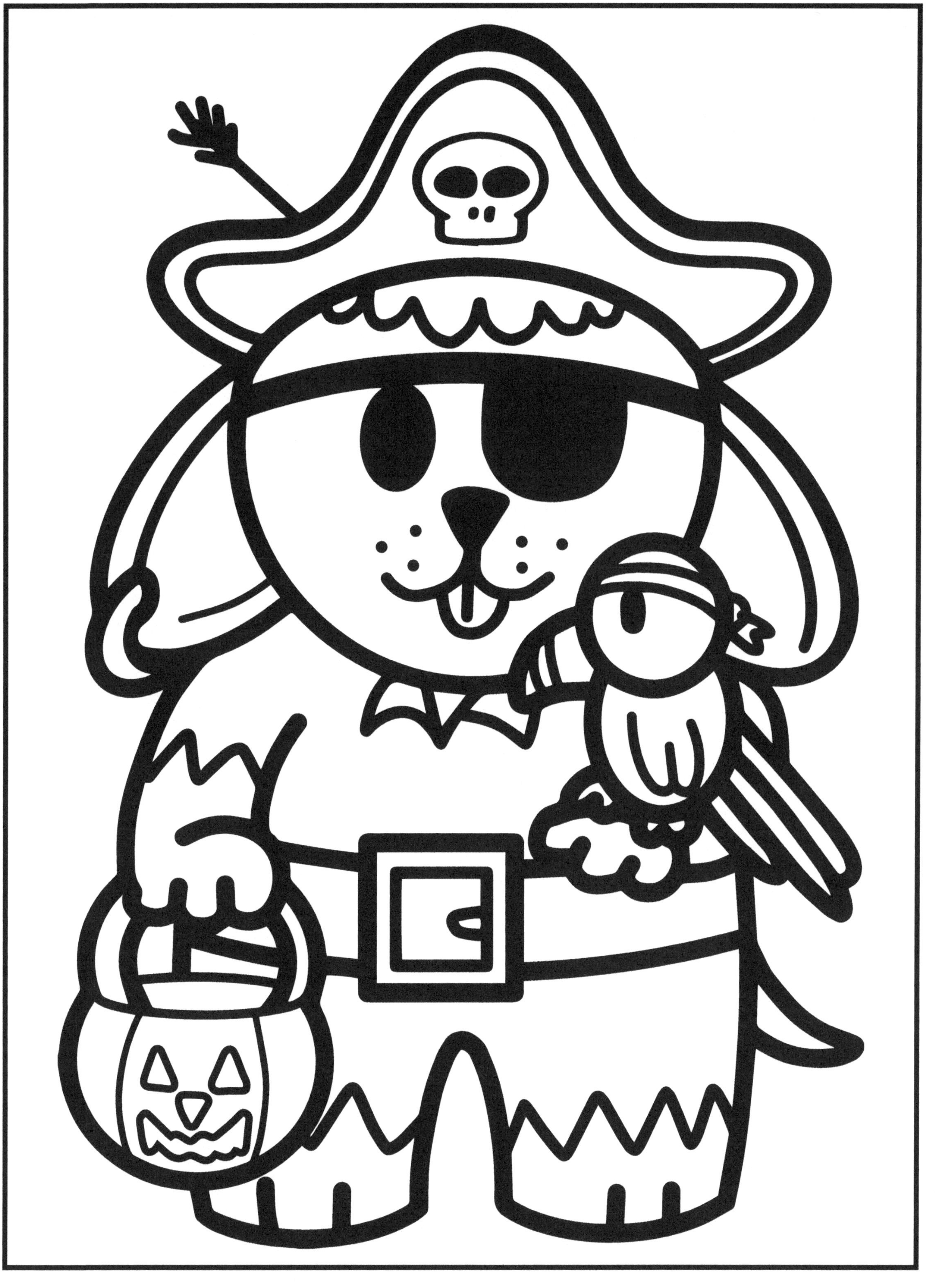

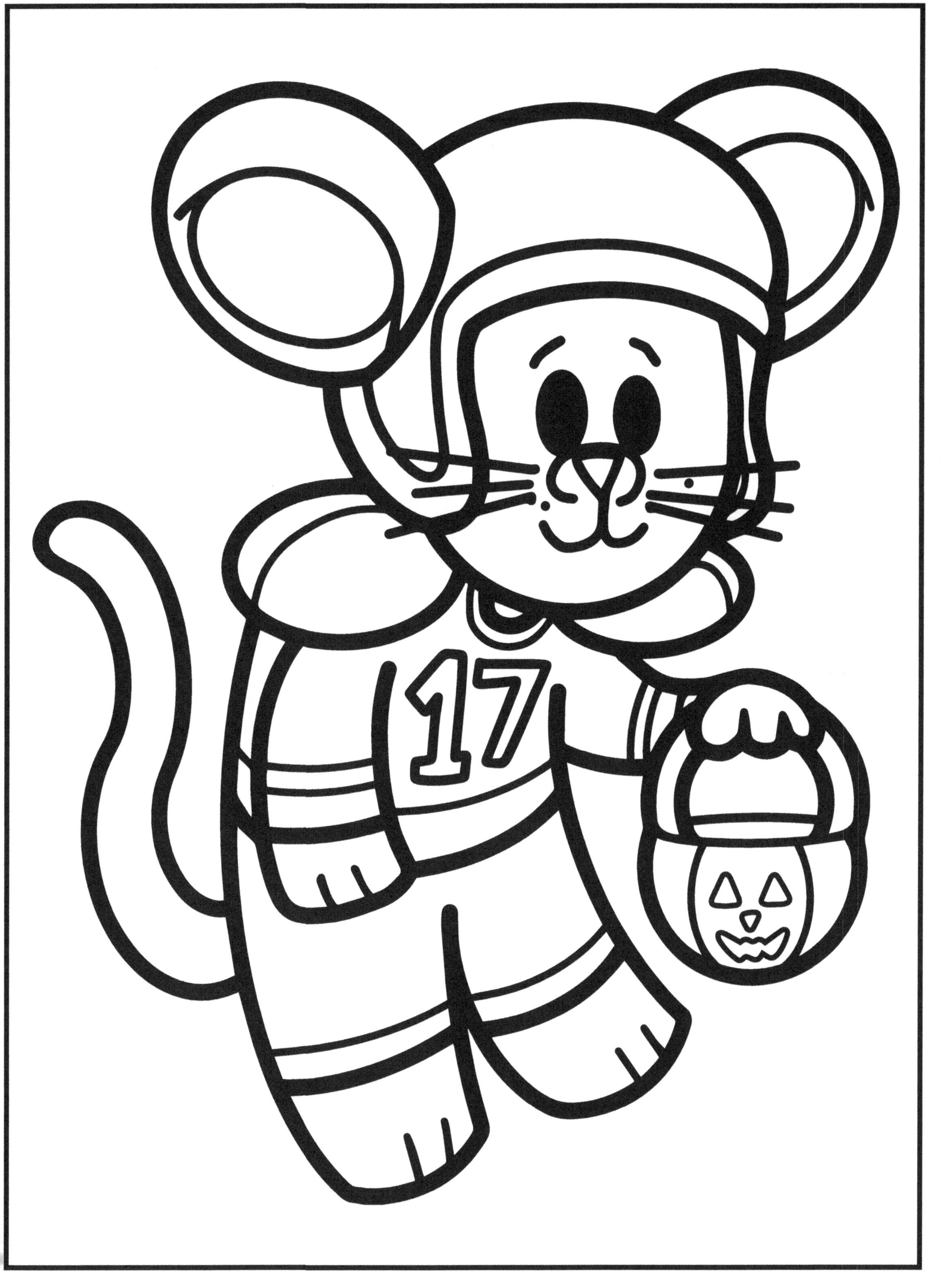
17

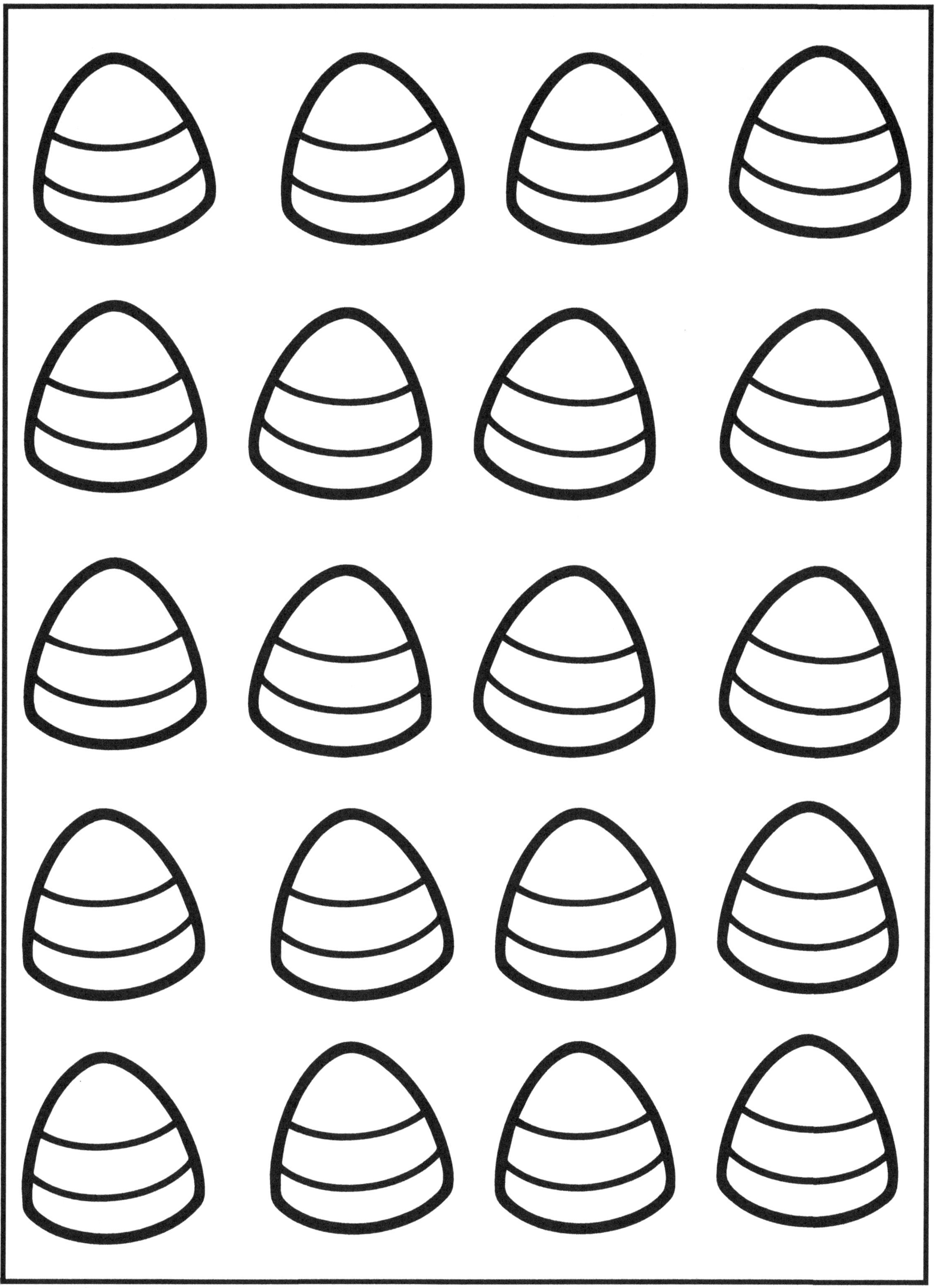

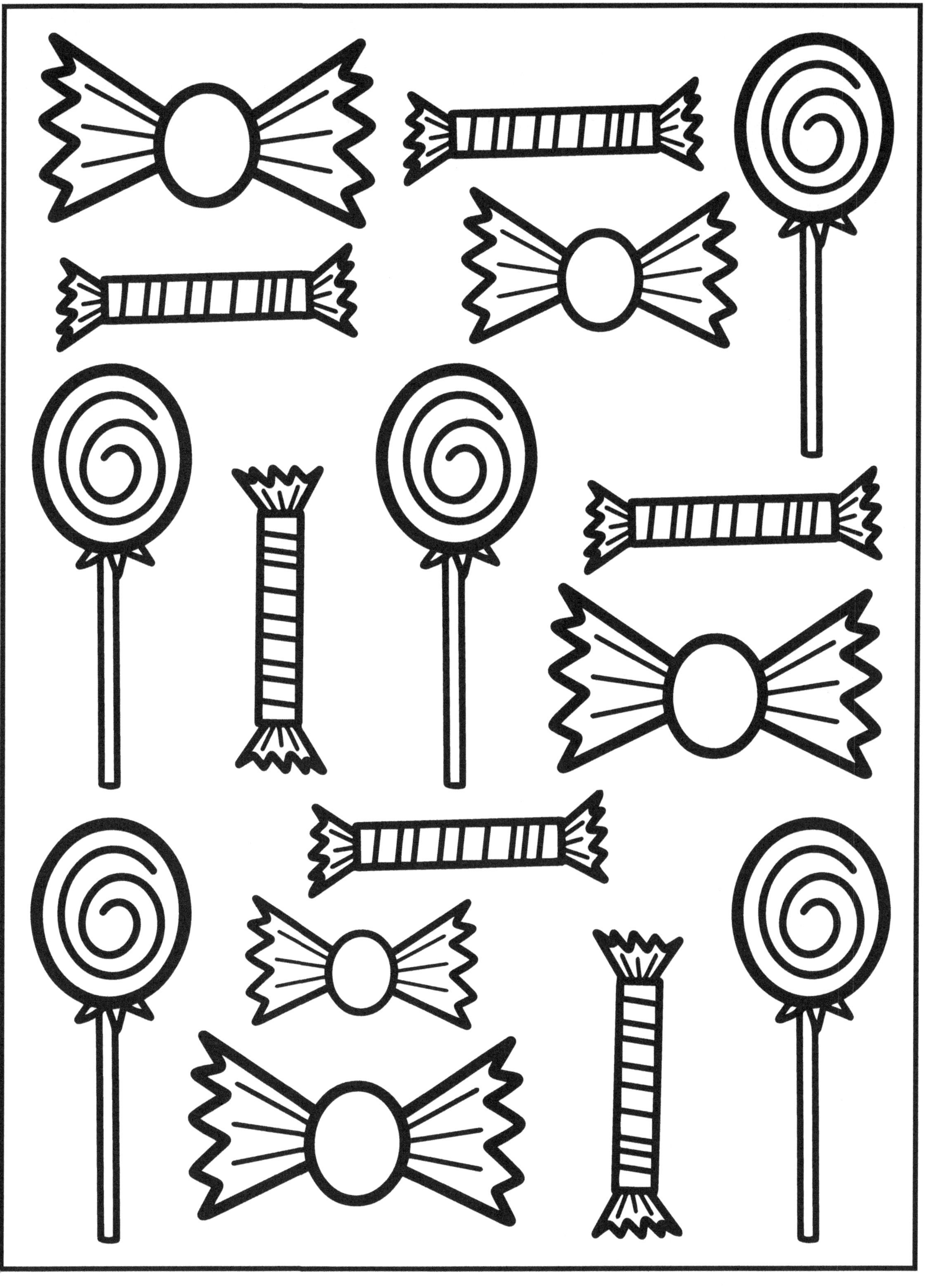

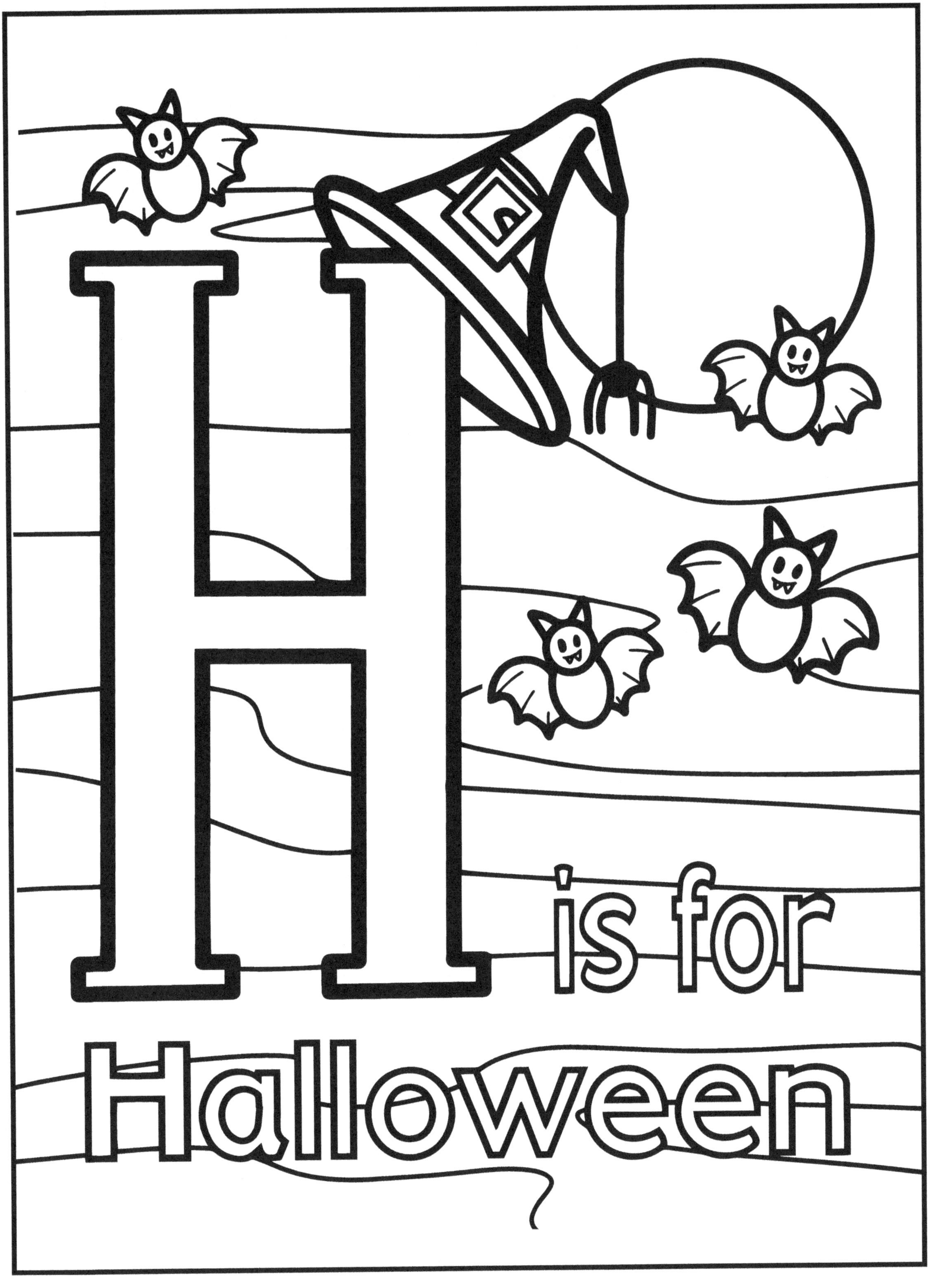
H
is for
Halloween

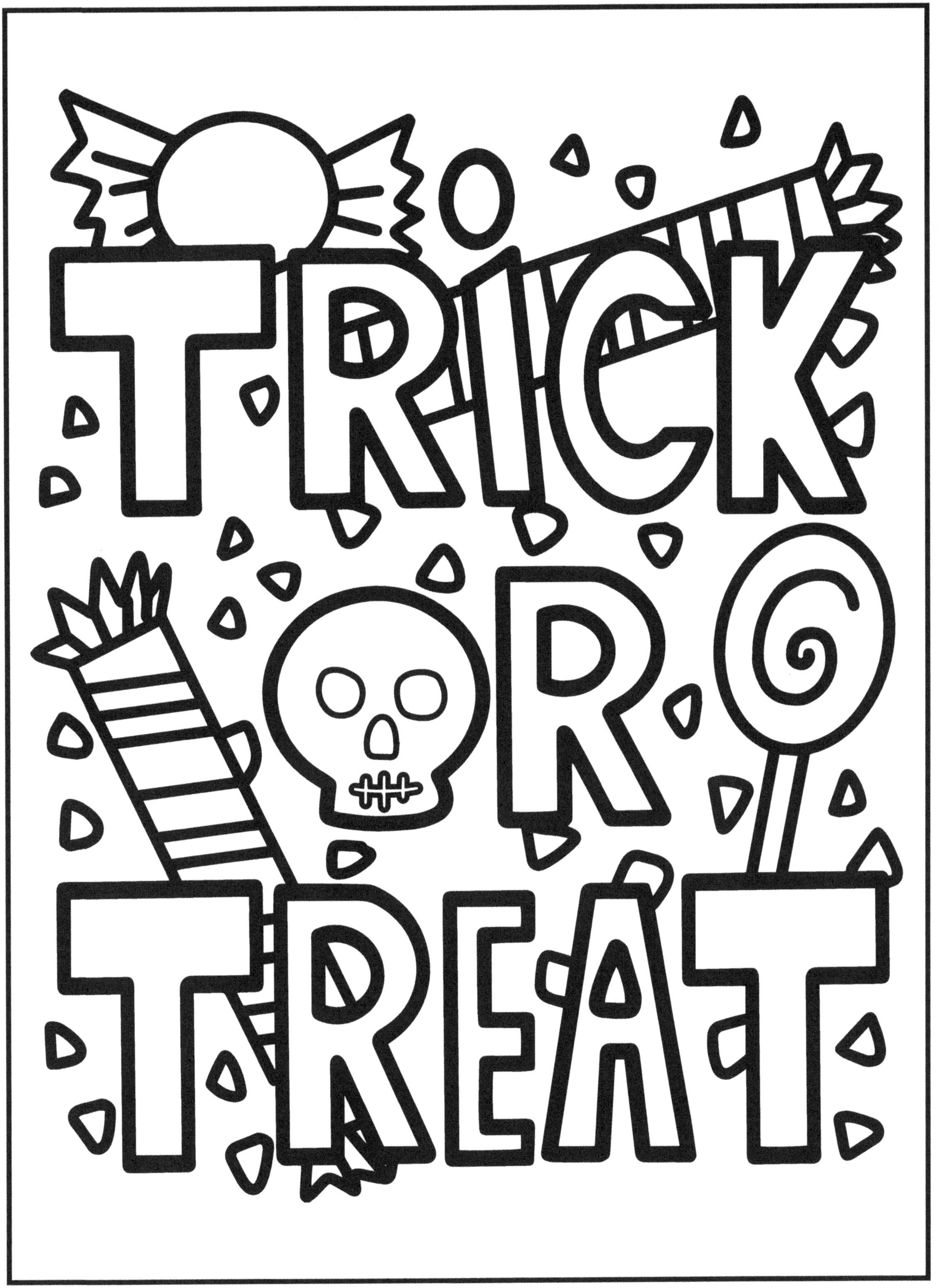
TRICK OR TREAT

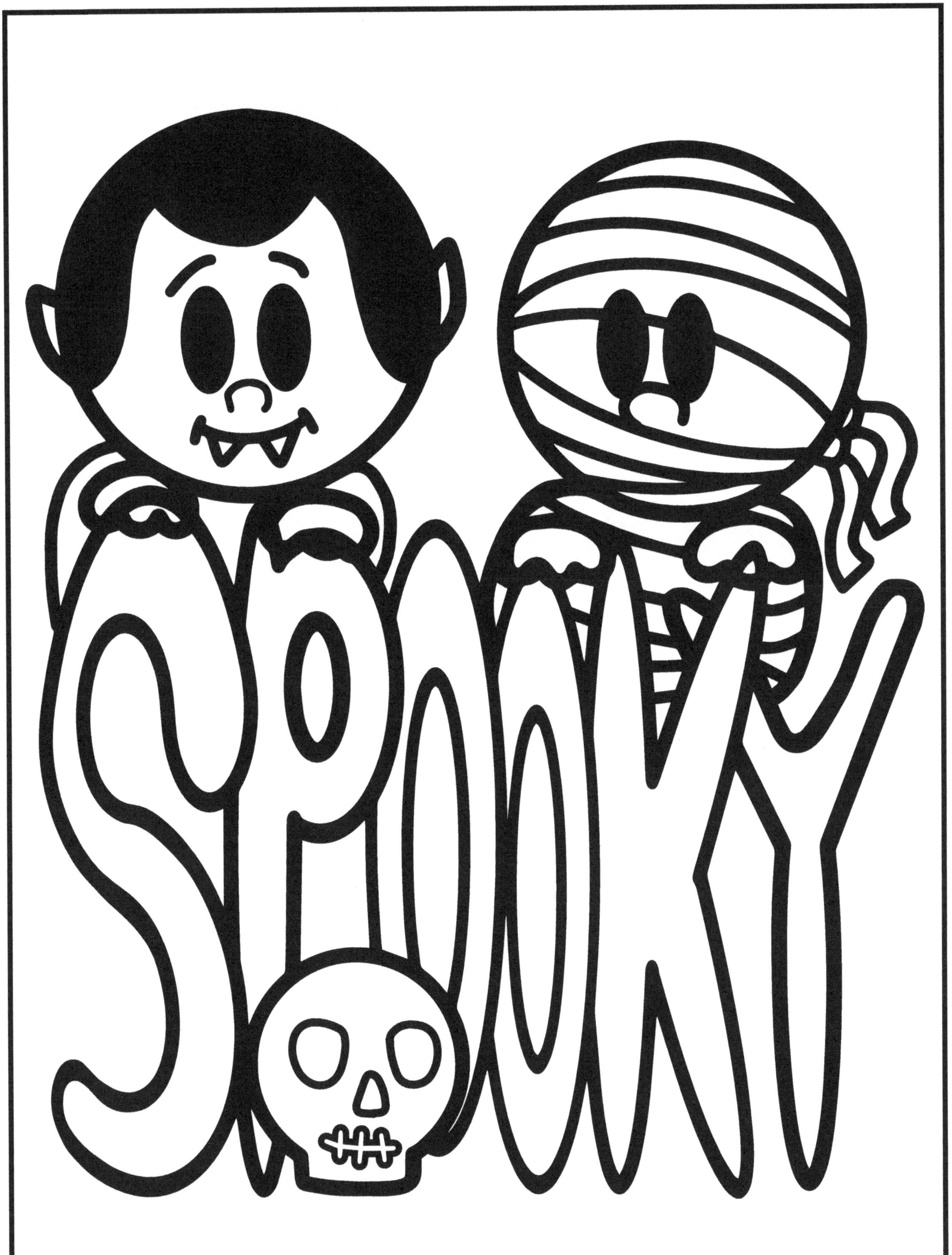
SPOOKY

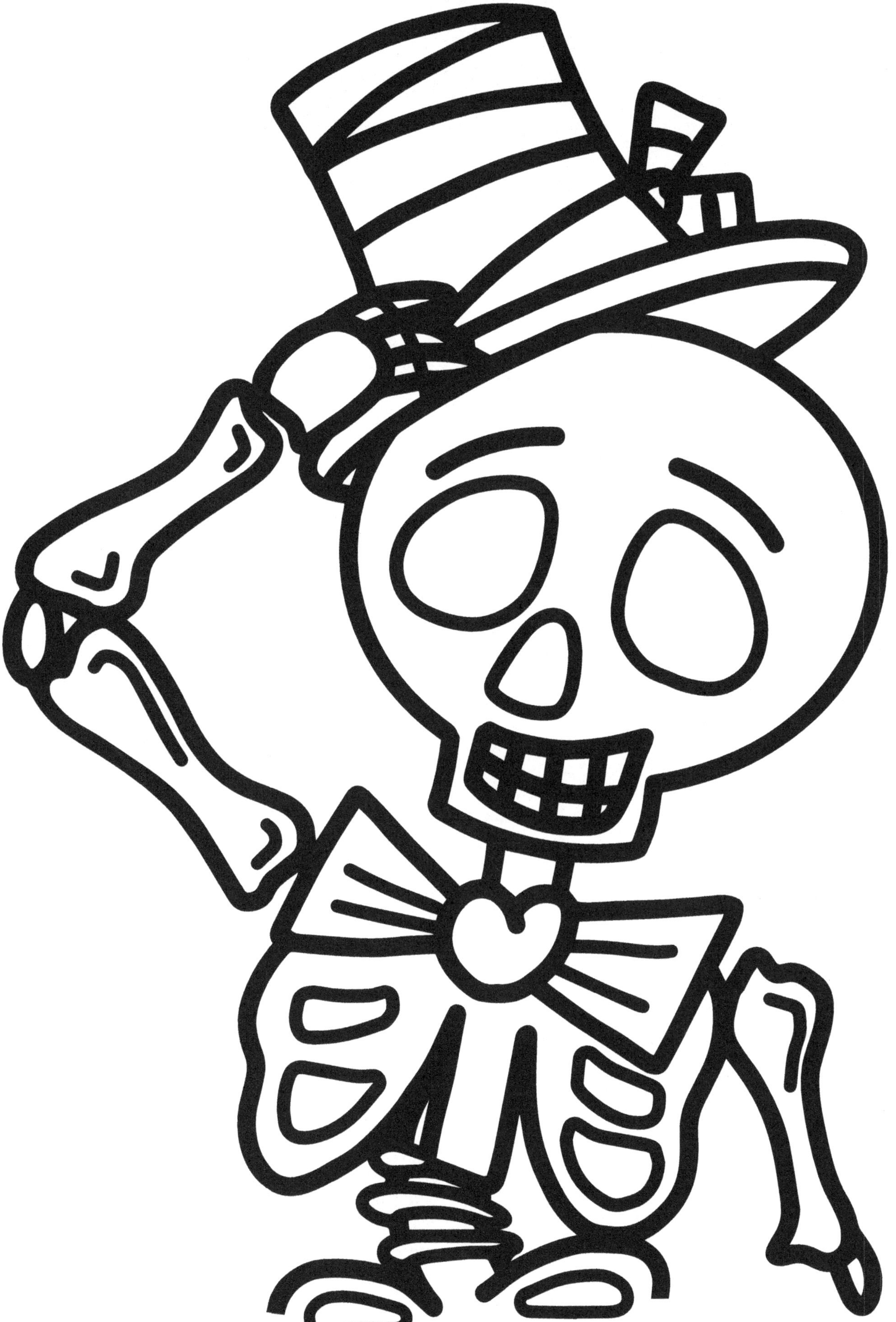

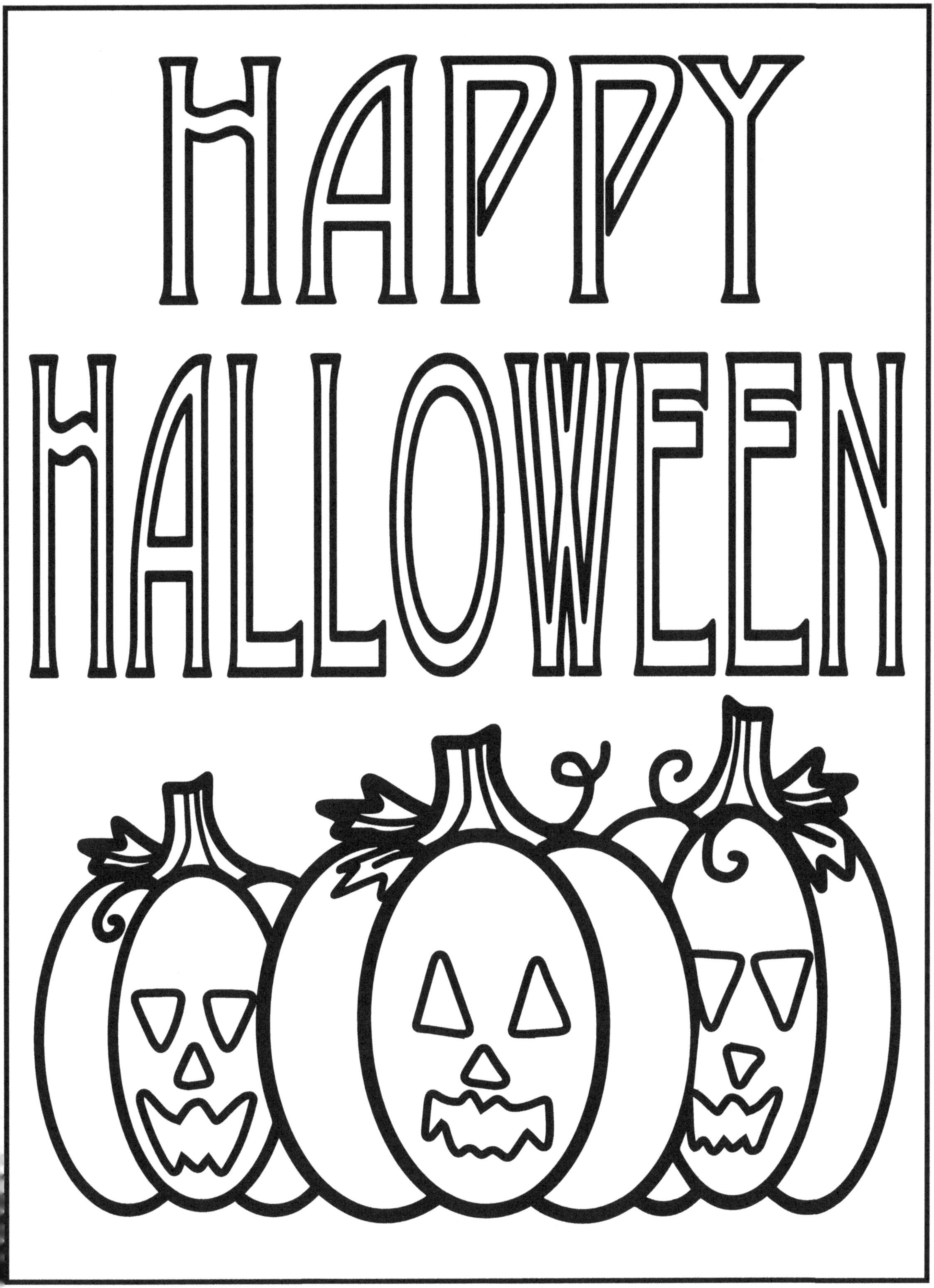
HAPPY
HALLOWEEN

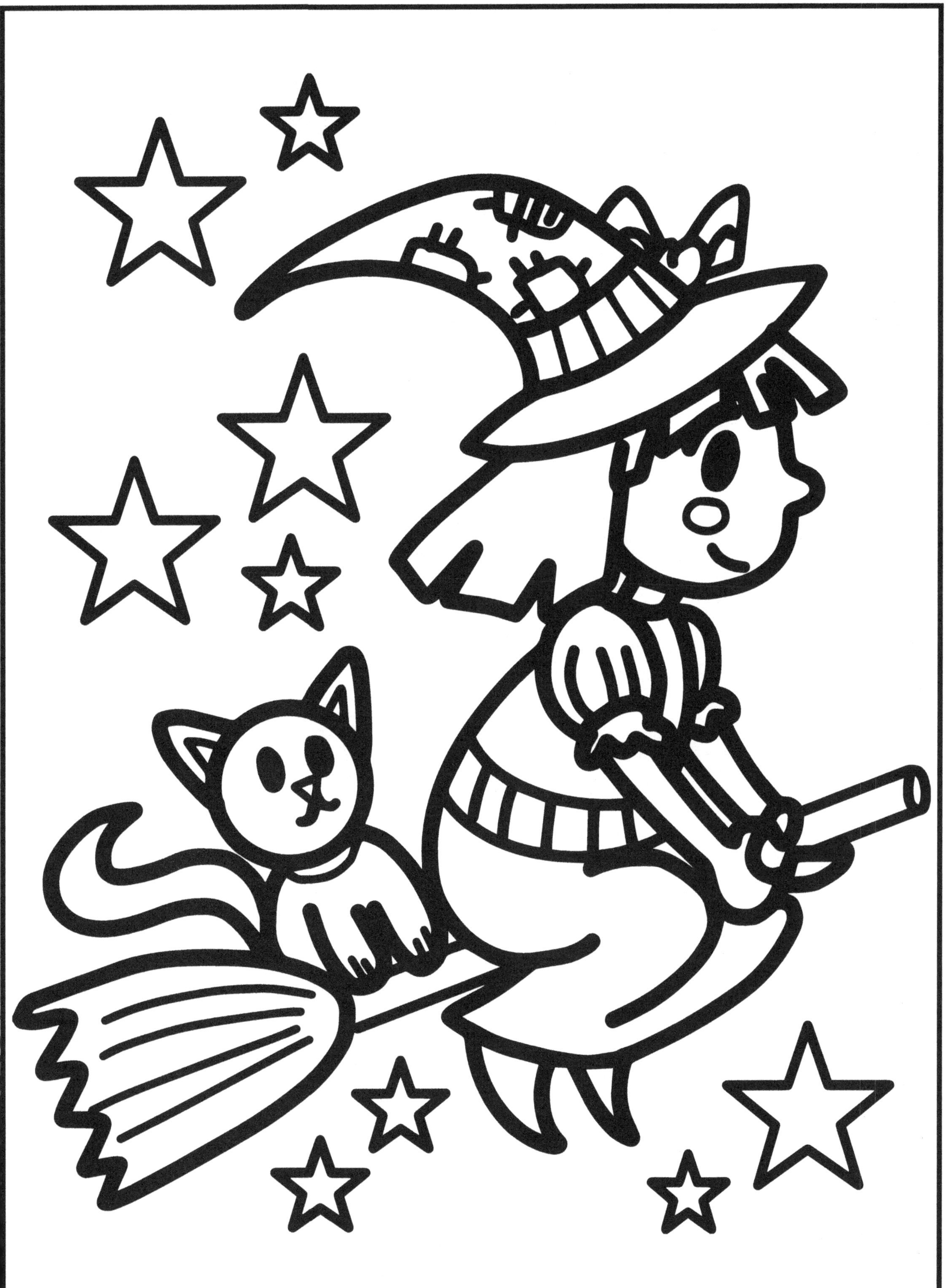

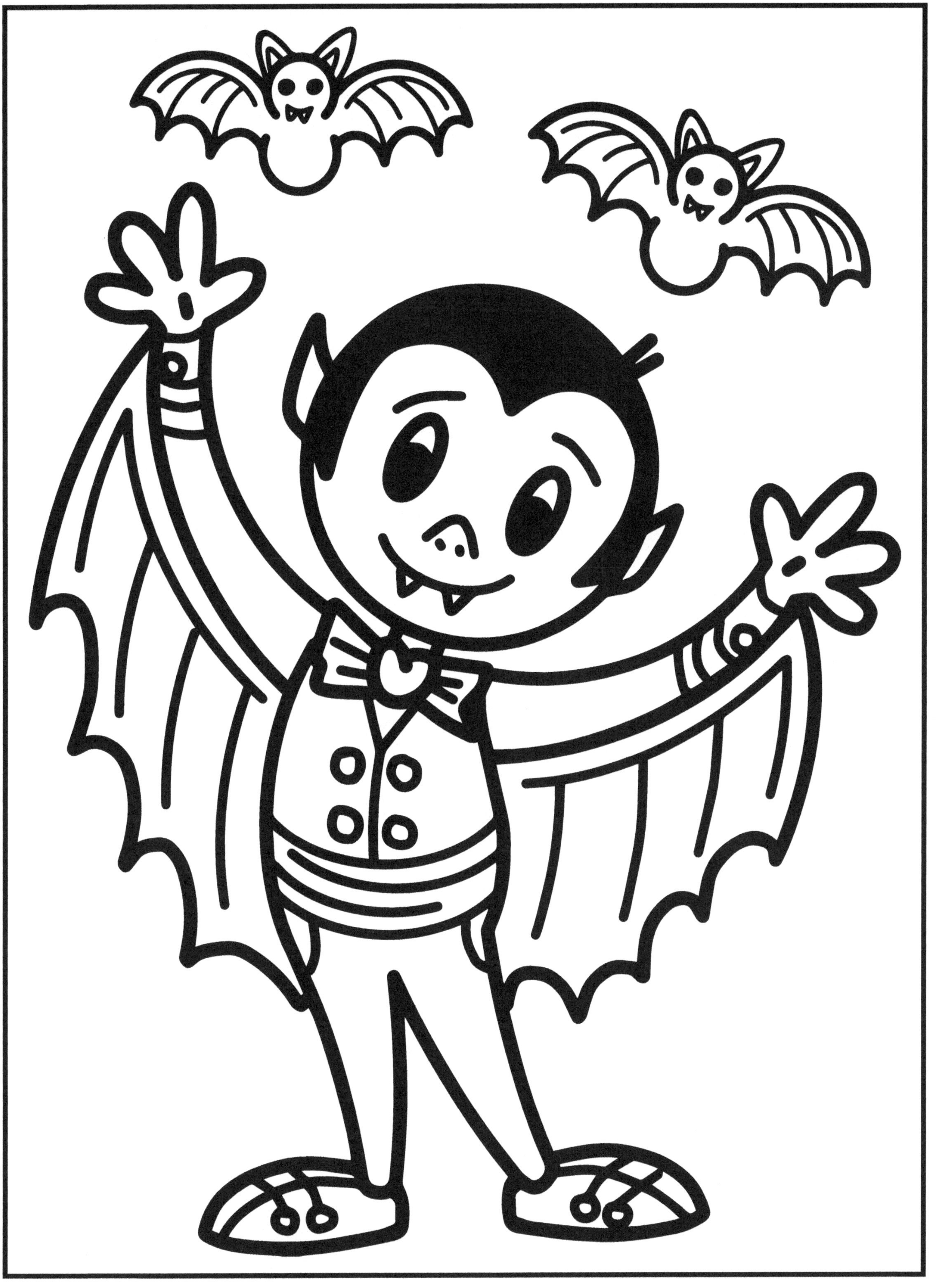

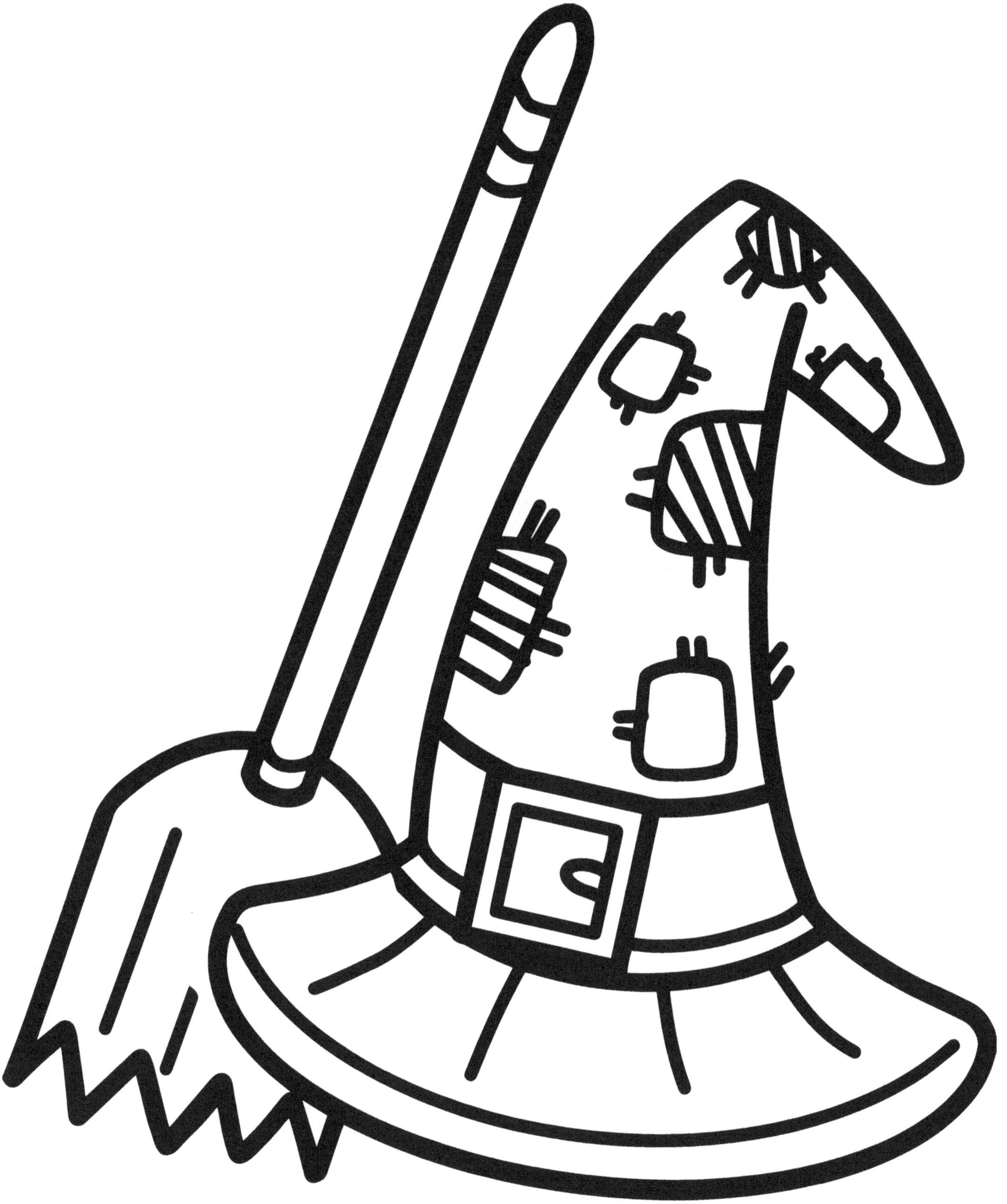

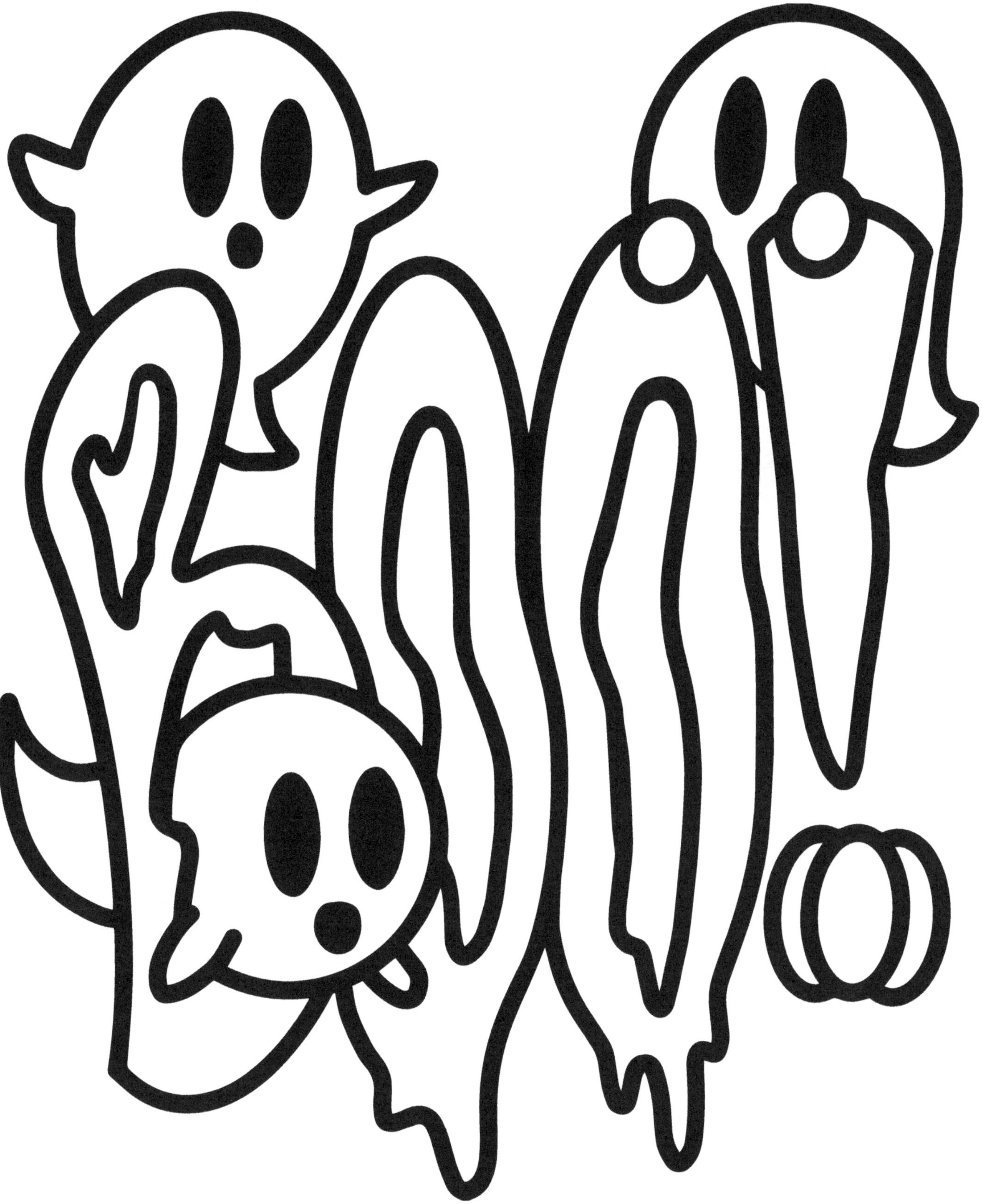
BOO!

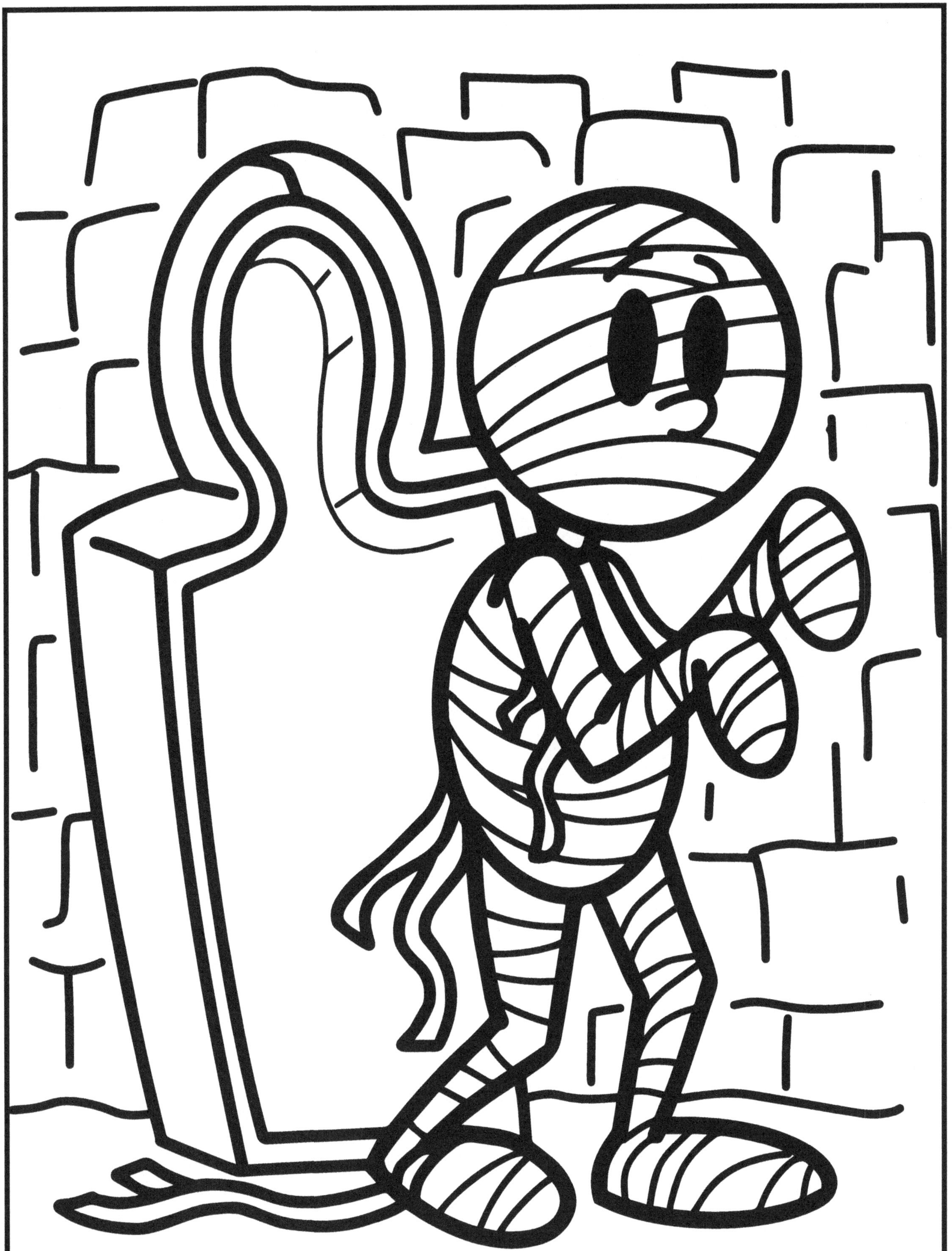

Made in the USA
Middletown, DE
14 October 2023

40791799R00051